East Brother

HISTORY
OF AN
ISLAND
LIGHT STATION

Frank Perry

———————————————— 1984 —

Published by
East Brother Light Station, Inc.
117 Park Place
Point Richmond, California 94801

East Brother Light Station, Inc., is a
non-profit corporation licensed by the
U.S. Coast Guard to restore and operate East Brother light station as a
public service. For information on
visiting East Brother, write to the
above mailing address or telephone
(415) 233-2385.

Cover photos copyright 1982 by Sue Montague.

East Brother

(Photo by Frank Perry)

Contents

Foreword

Saving East Brother Light Station and making it accessible for the public to enjoy was a labor of love for many people. The principal contributors are listed in the back of the book, and they, as well as the hundreds of others who also supported the project in smaller ways, can be justifiably proud of what their labors and donations have achieved.

This book was commissioned by the Board of Directors of East Brother Light Station, Inc., as a tribute to all who worked to make the project possible. But particularly, I would like to recognize the contributions of a few very special people: Lucretia Edwards and the women of the Contra Costa Shoreline Parks Committee who initially saved East Brother from destruction by successfully nominating it to the National Register of Historic Places; Commander Joseph Blackett and Wayne Wheeler of the Coast Guard who encouraged us and trusted us with government property; The Monday Morning Gang who continue to maintain and improve the island's facilities; and finally to Walter Fanning, engineer, carpenter, innkeeper, machinist, and skipper, who can do almost anything better than anyone I have ever known. His talents and dedication continue to be an inspiration to us all.

Thomas K. Butt
President, East Brother
Light Station, Inc.

7

Preface

This book was researched using primarily material gathered together by others during light station restoration. The greatest wealth of information about East Brother's past comes from Record Group 26, National Archives, Washington, D.C. Unfortunately, some of the old government records pertaining to this and other lighthouses were consumed by a Treasury Department fire in 1921. Nevertheless, enough has survived in the case of East Brother to document reasonably well its early history. Most helpful among these unpublished documents were the clipping file, topographical report dated 1882, correspondence file, descriptive pamphlet dated 1919, index to correspondence received by the Lighthouse Board, abstract of miscellaneous contracts made by the Lighthouse Board, the registers of lighthouse keepers' salaries, and the station journals.

Published United States government sources yielded information not only about East Brother, but also about the Lighthouse Service in general. Particularly useful were the annual reports of the Lighthouse Board and the Bureau of Lighthouses, the U.S. *Statutes at Large*, and early *Light Lists*. Other federal government publications consulted were: *Instructions and Directions to Guide Light-House Keepers and Others Belonging to the Light-House Establishment* (January 1, 1870); *Instructions to Light-Keepers* (July 1881); *The Modern Light-House Service* by Arnold Johnson (1890); *The United States Lighthouse Service* by John S. Conway (1923); and *The Lighthouse Service: Its History, Activities, and Organization* by George Weiss (1926).

East Brother's recent history is chronicled by the extensive collection of newspaper clippings, correspondence, and photographs preserved by East Brother Light Station, Inc. These were compiled from the collections of individuals as well as the files of many different local agencies and institutions.

Government publications, recent correspondence, and photographs were also examined at the U.S. Coast Guard, Twelfth District, Aids to Navigation Branch in Alameda, California. I am particularly indebted to Mr. Wayne Wheeler for kindly making these materials available to me and for his many helpful comments and suggestions for improving the manuscript.

In addition, I especially wish to thank the following for their help: Tom Butt; Walter Fanning; Leigh and Linda Hurley; Sally Legakis; McHenry Library, U.C. Santa Cruz; National Maritime Museum, San Francisco; Nancy Norton; Edith Perry; the Richmond Public Library; Suzanne Schettler; Ralph Shanks; David Shonman; Kirk and Pat Smith; and Nels Stenmark.

Frank Perry

Introduction

If one were to describe the "typical" lighthouse, it would probably be a tall, white, circular tower, made of brick or stone, with black trim and a few slender windows. It would be located on the open coast, warning ships of treacherous surf or dangerous rocks. Indeed, some of America's best known beacons fit this description: Cape Hatteras in North Carolina, Portland Head in Maine, and Pigeon Point on the central coast of California. Based on these criteria, East Brother light station would not be considered typical. Its lighthouse is a rectangular, wooden building, painted buff color with white trim. It is not especially tall, and it overlooks a bay instead of an ocean.

In reality, though, East Brother was not at all an unusual lighthouse during its heyday in the late nineteenth and early twentieth centuries. Several other lighthouses were built on the West Coast in the late 1800s using similar plans. It was also one of about a dozen lighthouses built on greater San Francisco Bay. Like other United States lighthouses, it was constructed and operated by the federal government, primarily as a nighttime aid to navigation.

Today, East Brother *is* unusual in that much of it has been restored to its early-day appearance and function. A giant cistern still stores rainwater for use on the island. Victorian-style trim decorates the outside of the dwelling and tower. And the mighty diaphone fog signal, installed in 1934, roars back to life to the thrill of visitors. Guests can even stay overnight, dining and sleeping where the different light-keepers lived for nearly one hundred years. Today, as a living museum, East Brother light station preserves an almost forgotten, yet important, part of America's maritime history.

East Brother Island is one of two tiny islands on the east side of San Pablo Strait, a two-mile-wide waterway connecting San Francisco Bay with San Pablo Bay. The island covers just three quarters of an acre. Neighboring West Brother, only a stone's throw away, is even smaller. The only inhabitants on West Brother are the flocks of gulls, cormorants, and pelicans that perch on its rounded, rocky crest. East Brother had similar inhabitants and a similar shape until 1873 when the federal government hired contractors to blast off the top of the island and begin constructing a light station.

The captains who guided ships through San Pablo Strait badly needed a lighthouse. The strait connects the Golden Gate, San Francisco, and other San Francisco Bay ports with inland ports such as Stockton and Sacramento. Ships traveling to and from the Mare Island Navy Yard must also pass through these waters. Vessels that stray off course at night or in fog could easily collide with the numerous rocky islands and nearby shoals.

The lighthouse, originally a six-room dwelling with an attached tower for the light, was built at the west end of the island. The government also had the workers construct a fog signal building, workshop, wharf, boathouse, water tanks, cistern, and rain catchment basin. Since the station was only accessible by boat, it was equipped so that the keepers could meet most any sudden demand, be it high winds, storm waves, or unexpected equipment failures.

About three dozen different men served at East Brother through the years as keepers and assistants. They faithfully kept the light burning each night, guiding ships across the bay waters. Many of the keepers lived there with their families, who in later years recalled with nostalgia their days

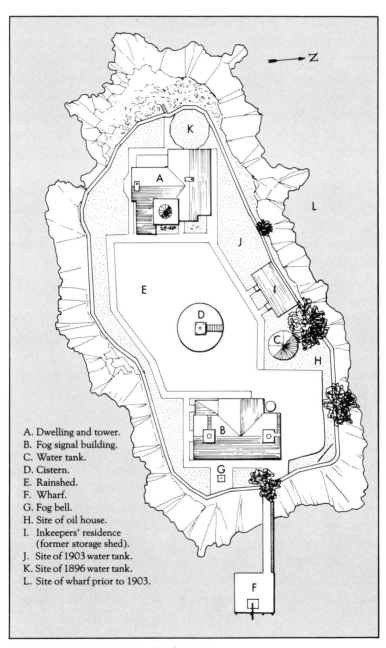

A. Dwelling and tower.
B. Fog signal building.
C. Water tank.
D. Cistern.
E. Rainshed.
F. Wharf.
G. Fog bell.
H. Site of oil house.
I. Inkeepers' residence
   (former storage shed).
J. Site of 1903 water tank.
K. Site of 1896 water tank.
L. Site of wharf prior to 1903.

Map of East Brother Island.

on the island. It was a peaceful life, away from the mainland rush, yet a life with a special sense of duty and fulfillment.

Though the station was in many ways isolated from the mainland, the world did not pass it by. As technology and the lighthouse administration changed, so did operation of East Brother. In 1934 electricity replaced kerosene as energy for the light. That same year compressed air replaced steam as power for the fog signal. In later years rotating crews of Coast Guardsmen replaced the keepers of the old U.S. Lighthouse Service.

In the late 1960s technology brought what was nearly the final chapter in the station's history. The Coast Guard decided to automate East Brother. To save on salaries and maintenance costs, an automatic rotating beacon was installed in the lighthouse, and the last resident personnel said goodbye to their island home. Coast Guard officials had announced that the old buildings would eventually be demolished and a light placed on a steel or concrete tower. This, they said, would be easier to maintain and less prone to vandalism. The announcement angered many local citizens; they dearly loved the quaint old landmark and vowed to save it.

In 1971, primarily through the efforts of the Contra Costa Shoreline Parks Committee, the station was placed on the National Register of Historic Places. This protected it from being razed, but neither the Coast Guard nor other public agencies had funds for maintaining or restoring the buildings. For ten years the birds and natural elements reclaimed the island. The only people who regularly visited it were Coast Guard service crews who periodically checked the light and electronic fog signal. In the meantime the paint peeled, the iron rusted, and the wood rotted.

In 1979 East Brother Light Station, Inc., a non-profit citizens' group, was formed with the goal of restoring the landmark and making it available for public use. The organization successfully applied for a Maritime Preservation Matching Grant from the U.S. Department of the Interior. The Coast Guard enthusiastically supported the project and gave the organization a license to occupy the island. With the help of private donations and hundreds of volunteers, the lighthouse and other island structures were restored and rehabilitated. The equivalent of $300,000 was put into the project, which was completed in 1980. Today, day use fees, operation as a bed and breakfast inn, and continued volunteer help make upkeep and further restoration possible.

Unfortunately, many of California's lighthouses have not been so lucky. Of the nearly fifty lighthouses that were built to watch over California's seacoast and bays, fully a third either no longer exist or have been so altered as to spoil much of their aesthetic and historical value. This gives added importance to East Brother, where not only the lighthouse but the entire station is preserved. Several relatives and descendants of early keepers have shared their remembrances of life on the island. The station journals have also survived, giving virtually a daily record of events at the station from first lighting in 1874 through 1945. All this makes the story of East Brother light station an unusually rich, well documented, and personal history.

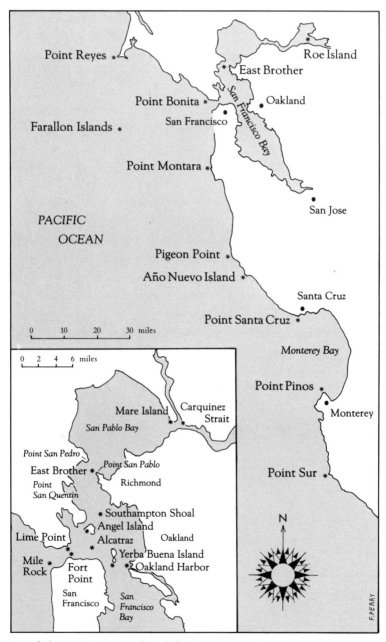

Lighthouses in central California, past and present.

West Coast Lighthouses

East Brother was one of about seventy lighthouses built on the West Coast of the United States in the late 1800s and early 1900s. Its history is linked to these other beacons in many ways. All were built and maintained by the federal government. All responded to similar changes in our culture and technology. And many were cared for by keepers who had worked at other lighthouses as well. In other respects, however, each lighthouse, including East Brother, has its own unique story to tell.

Lighthouses help mariners in several ways. Major sea coast lights serve as landfalls for ships arriving from across the ocean. These lighthouses and the smaller lights along the coast and in bays also act as guides for coastal vessels, in some cases warning them of dangerous reefs or shoals. Others mark turning points along the coast or at entrances to bays or harbors.

Most also aid mariners as landmarks visible during the day. They are, however, of little help day or night when there is thick fog. In the past many light stations were equipped with a fog signal such as a bell, steam whistle, or steam siren. Today such devices have given way to electronic fog signals and radio beacons. These modern aids and ship-based radar have frequently made lighthouses of secondary importance in navigation. Nevertheless, there is still nothing quite as reassuring as seeing a light, particularly when steering a vessel near shore to enter a harbor or bay.

Several events shaped the early history of West Coast

lighthouses. These in turn set the stage for construction of later stations such as at East Brother Island. First was the acquisition by the United States of Oregon Territory in 1846 and California in 1848. No lighthouses were built in California under Spain or Mexico. Lighthouses would have been of little benefit since so few ships served the small population in Alta California at that time. There is a report that the Spaniards sometimes hung a lantern on a stake at Ballast Point when a ship was expected at San Diego Bay, but this was hardly a lighthouse. Thus the United States started from scratch in planning a system of lighthouses for the Pacific Coast.

Another dramatic event, the discovery of gold in 1848, changed the face of California almost overnight. Hundreds of ships, each filled with hopeful gold-seekers, set sail for the Golden Gate. The gold rush touched off continued immigration which brought growth in agriculture, lumbering, construction and other activities. As cities and towns swelled with activity, so did commerce and shipping. California's population of immigrants grew from less than 15,000 in early 1848 to 223,856 in 1852.[1] By 1870 the state's population had expanded to over 560,000.[2]

The third significant event in the early development of West Coast lighthouses was the establishment of the Lighthouse Board. This administrative body took over the duties of the fifth auditor of the Treasury Department, who had supervised the nation's lighthouse system from 1820 to 1852. On August 31, 1852, Congress passed an act requiring the President to appoint three high ranking officers from the Navy, three engineers from the Army, and two civilian scientists to constitute the Lighthouse Board. The Secretary of Treasury served as the board's *ex-officio* president.

The diverse makeup of the Lighthouse Board enabled it more easily to administer the varied duties of a growing lighthouse establishment, which included maintaining lightships, buoys, fog signals and other navigational aids. The board intended to improve the quality and dependability of United States lighthouses, bringing them up to the level of those in France, England, and Scotland.

The Lighthouse Board held its first meeting October 9, 1852. One of its early tasks was to divide the nation into twelve lighthouse districts. The entire West Coast became the Twelfth District with headquarters in San Francisco. (Later Oregon and Washington were made into the Thirteenth District.) Each district had a Naval officer as an inspector in charge of personnel and daily operations, and an Army engineer to oversee new construction and repairs at the different light stations. The Lighthouse Board planned most of the lighthouses eventually built on the West Coast, but not all. By the time they met, arrangements had already been made to construct the first set of lighthouses here.

Earlier, on April 20, 1852, the government contracted with the firm of Francis A. Gibbons and Francis X. Kelly of Baltimore, Maryland, to build eight lighthouses. These were to be constructed at Point Loma near San Diego, Point Conception, Point Pinos near Monterey, Southeast Farallon Island, Battery Point (Fort Point) and Alcatraz Island on San Francisco Bay, and at Humboldt Harbor—all in California. They were also hired to build a lighthouse at Cape Disappointment at the mouth of the Columbia River in what is now Washington.

Gibbons and Kelly purchased the bark *Oriole,* gave her new fittings, and loaded the ship with all materials necessary to build the lighthouses with the exception of stone, which would be quarried near each lighthouse site. The shipload of materials with crew and workmen set sail from Baltimore August 12, 1852, and arrived in San Francisco on January 29, 1853.[3] Gibbons and Kelly agreed to build the eight lighthouses for just $136,000—all that Congress had appropriated.

From early on the builders were plagued by unexpected

difficulties. Just three months after the Battery Point lighthouse was constructed (but before the lens arrived from France), the Army selected that very site for a fort. The structure was razed before ever being lighted, and eventually a second lighthouse was built. After construction of lighthouses at Battery Point, Alcatraz, Point Pinos, and Southeast Farallon Island, the workmen sailed north to Cape Disappointment. The site was aptly named. Here the *Oriole* was wrecked and her cargo destroyed. Fortunately, no lives were lost, but work was delayed while replacement materials were purchased. At Point Loma the problems continued. Additional time and materials needed to build a road to the site made the cost nearly double the $15,000 originally budgeted for the job.[4] At Point Conception and Southeast Farallon Island the lighthouses had to be rebuilt because the lenses, when they arrived, were too big to fit. Finally, on June 1, 1854, the Alcatraz Island lighthouse became the first to be lighted on the West Coast. Not until October of 1856 did the last of these first eight lighthouses, Cape Disappointment, go into operation.

Each lighthouse was a simple, rectangular, masonry dwelling known as a Cape Cod structure. Most had a circular tower rising from the center, though at several locations the on-site decision was made to offset the tower or detach it from the dwelling. The design was devised by Ammi B. Young, an architect employed by the Treasury Department.[5]

By the end of the 1850s eight more lighthouses were built on the West Coast. They were similar in design to the first eight, but were built by local contractors and for even less money than the amount paid to Gibbons and Kelly. The second eight were built at Santa Barbara, Point Bonita, and Crescent City in California, at Umpqua River in Oregon, and at Willapa Bay, Cape Flattery, Smith Island, and New Dungeness in Washington.

During the early 1860s, while the nation was preoccupied with the Civil War, no lighthouses were built on the West Coast. In fact, during the war 164 East Coast lights were discontinued and many were badly damaged.[6] By 1866, however, most of these beacons had been repaired and relighted, and the Lighthouse Board again turned its attention to constructing new lighthouses.

In the 1850s and 1860s the Pacific's ragged edge devoured numerous ships. The loss of these vessels, their cargo, and many lives underscored the need for additional lighthouses. In California during the late 1860s and early 1870s twelve more lighthouses, many with fog signals, would be constructed—among these East Brother.

A Light Station
for
East Brother

San Francisco Bay ranks among the world's great natural harbors. Though the Golden Gate at its narrowest point is but a mile wide, it opens into a bay covering nearly 450 square miles. The bay has not one harbor but dozens along its one hundred miles of meandering shoreline.

San Francisco Bay proper stretches from Alviso near San Jose in the south to points San Pablo and San Pedro in the north. Between these two points lies San Pablo Strait. The two islands called The Brothers mark the east side of the strait, a quarter mile off point San Pablo. On the west side are two similar islands named The Sisters. It is not known who named these two sets of islands nor when they were named. It has long been a tradition, however, to name two or more similarly-shaped islands or mountains in this way. Two islands also called The Brothers lie just south of Cape Mendocino in Humboldt County. The names for the San Francisco Bay islands became official in 1851 when the U.S. Coast Survey used them in preparing the first accurate map of the bay.

Besides providing shelter for boats, San Francisco and San Pablo bays also link the vast Sacramento and San Joaquin river systems to the Pacific Ocean. Much of the river water comes from melted snow in the Sierra Nevada, and some of it flows as much as four hundred miles before reaching the ocean. During the Gold Rush, the Sacramento and San Joaquin rivers were important transportation routes, helping link San Francisco with the Sierra. In the 1850s and 1860s dozens of boats regularly ferried mail, passengers, and freight between San Francisco and inland ports as far north as Red Bluff and nearly as far south as Fresno.[7] By the 1870s railroads started taking much of the business away from the river boats, but even today freighters unload and pick up cargo at Sacramento—a hundred miles inland from the sea.

In 1854, when the federal government established a Navy shipyard at Mare Island near Vallejo, ship traffic through San Pablo Strait further increased. By 1866 the Mare Island fleet numbered nearly 700 ships.[8]

In response to the continued growth of the San Francisco Bay area, three sites overlooking the bay waters were recognized in the early 1870s as needing lighthouses and fog signals. These were Yerba Buena Island between San Francisco and Oakland, the east side of San Pablo Strait, and the southern tip of Mare Island.

Previously, in 1851, the Coast Survey had anchored a marker buoy over Invincible Rock, a submerged hazard about one half mile southwest of The Brothers. By the early 1870s other buoys marked hazards bordering the strait, but ship captains who regularly navigated these waters needed a better guide at night and during fog. On March 3, 1871, Congress appropriated $20,000 for construction of a lighthouse and fog signal for this purpose.

After passage of the bill, lighthouse engineers examined land at Point San Pablo and tried to negotiate with the land owners for purchase of a suitable site on the mainland. The owners, however, refused to sell. This left the government with no choice other than to file suit against them for condemnation of the land. In July, 1871, at a special proceeding of the state Fifteenth District Court, the jury awarded the land owners $4,000 for the 12.8 acres wanted by the government. The Lighthouse Board thought that this judgment of the land's value was excessive, but being anxious to begin lighthouse construction, accepted the ruling. The owners of the land apparently thought this was not enough, so they appealed the case to the California Supreme Court.

In March of 1872 Paul J. Pelz, chief draftsman for the Lighthouse Board, went ahead and executed drawings for the proposed Point San Pablo lighthouse. He prepared them under the direction of Major George Elliot, engineering secretary of the board. In the meantime, litigation dragged on over the Point San Pablo site. The final hearing in the case was scheduled for October, but the defendants succeeded in delaying matters still further.

Soon two years had passed since plans were first made for a lighthouse along San Pablo Strait, and mariners who regularly traveled this route were growing impatient with the delays. In January, 1873, a number of captains from steamers and other vessels presented a petition to the lighthouse inspector in San Francisco urging that the lighthouse be built instead on nearby East Brother Island since the federal government already owned this property. The inspector agreed and on January 28 forwarded the petition to the Lighthouse Board for consideration.

The Lighthouse Board responded enthusiastically to the new site proposal. Besides avoiding the legal problems, having the light on the island would increase its arc of useful visibility and place it closer to shipping lanes. The primary disadvantages of the site would be the lack of fresh water for household use and operation of a steam-powered fog signal, the necessity of providing boat transportation, and the lack of adequate space for a keepers' garden.

The Brothers and The Sisters had been reserved for military purposes by President Andrew Johnson in 1867. At that time the islands were still unclaimed. Johnson had been advised that it might someday be necessary to erect batteries on these islands in the event enemy ships tried to reach Mare Island Navy Yard during a war.

The Treasury Secretary wrote to the Secretary of War

requesting permission to build a light and fog signal station on East Brother. The Secretary of War granted a fifty-year lease under the condition that the station "... shall give way to fortifications whenever it shall be required for that purpose."[9] He added, however, that it was not likely that these islands would be needed as sites for batteries for many years, if at all.*

In January, 1873, Twelfth District Assistant Lighthouse Engineer E. J. Molera landed on East Brother to draw a detailed map of the island to forward to the board. Molera saw that there would indeed be a problem getting enough fresh water to operate a steam engine for a fog whistle. Water would have to be shipped in or rainwater captured. This inspired Molera to propose to the Lighthouse Board his own design of a fog signal powered by compressed air instead of steam.

His plan called for excavating a 50-by-100-foot seawater reservoir in the middle of the island. A brass trumpet would then be fastened on top of a wooden platform above the reservoir. Seawater would be pumped into the reservoir by means of a "wave ram," a "tide mill," and an ordinary windmill. Exactly how all this would work is not clear, but the basic principle was that rising water level in the reservoir would compress air in a chamber to blow the trumpet.

Actually, the idea was not so far-fetched. In the 1860s Major Hartman Bache, then inspector for the same district, devised a fog whistle powered by compressed air from a natural blowhole above a sea cave. The signal ran for a number of years on Southeast Farallon Island and brought widespread acclaim to its inventor.

By 1873 steam whistles similar to those on locomotives and steamboats had come into common use as fog signals. Molera,

*In 1924 title was transferred to the Commerce Department (Bureau of Lighthouses) and later to the Coast Guard.

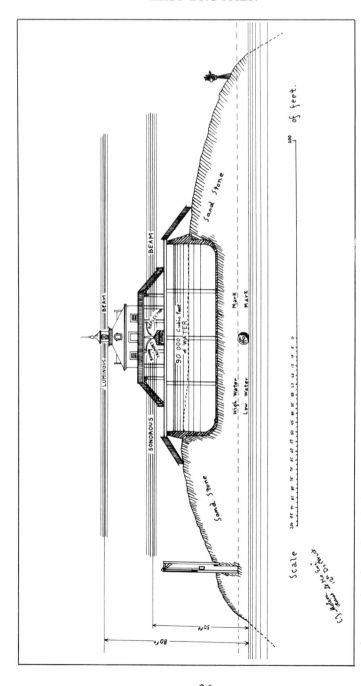

These early plans for a light station on East Brother were drafted by Assistant Lighthouse Engineer E. J. Molera and were never used. (U.S. Coast Guard)

however, compiled an impressive list of advantages his signal would have over steam whistles in addition to not requiring fresh water. It would not use any fuel and consequently there would also be less danger of fire—particularly hazardous on such a small island. It would require fewer people to operate and could be started instantaneously, unlike steam whistles which required time for the boiler to build up pressure. Also, the trumpet sound would less likely be confused with the whistles used on passing steamers. Molera planned to fix a sounding board and reflector to the device to help give it an intensity "superior to any yet produced."[10] The lighthouse would be located above the trumpet to help focus the sound horizontally. Apparently the impact of this on the keepers was not considered.

Molera waited anxiously for a response to his proposal. In the meantime, on March 3, 1873, Congress appropriated an additional $30,000 for construction of a lighthouse and fog signal for San Pablo Strait. In April the government withdrew its condemnation suit and proceeded with plans to erect the station on East Brother Island. Despite Molera's list of advantages, the Lighthouse Board did not implement his plan. It was untested and the delays in securing the site now left little time for such experimentation. Instead they decided to use the lighthouse plan already drafted (originally intended for Point San Pablo) and construct a steam-powered fog whistle on the island.

In May, 1873, requests were sent out for bids to grade the site and build the lighthouse and fog signal building. On July 24 the firm of Monroe and Burns of San Francisco was hired for the sum of $17,637.65.

The contractors immediately began blasting sandstone from the top of the island. Some of the sandstone was used to build a wall around the island's perimeter. More of the center of the island was then leveled and used to fill in behind the wall, thus creating about one half acre of level ground for the station.

Several changes in the lighthouse plans were made to accommodate the new site. The front of the lighthouse was originally to face west towards the bay. It was made to face east instead, towards the rest of the island. A two-room cellar originally planned was omitted.

The design for the lighthouse, rich in gingerbread and scrollwork, was typical of the 1860s and 1870s. The porches, wide overhangs, and sawn banisters were characteristic of the "seaside cottages" illustrated in architectural pattern books widely distributed at that time. The Lighthouse Board's policy was to build simple and substantial dwellings that would be appropriate to the purpose yet in harmony with the prevailing local architecture. As with the first set of lighthouses built on the West Coast, the plans used at East Brother were also used, with modifications, at several other locations. In the early 1870s lighthouses similar in design to East Brother were built at Point Fermin, Point Hueneme, and Mare Island in California, and at Point Adams in Oregon. Of these, only Point Fermin near Los Angeles stands today.

By the fall of 1873 the lighthouse foundation was in place and the walls were going up. It was basically a six-room dwelling, yet was intended as quarters for three keepers— two with families. It was definitely the kind of arrangement that encouraged one to try to get along with the neighbors. A bedroom and living room for the principal keeper were downstairs. Upstairs were another bedroom and living room. A third keeper would live in the garret, above the communal kitchen and dining room. Stairs inside and outside connected the two levels, and both levels had closets and storerooms.

The lighthouse was built of wood, but with an unusual feature. The spaces between the studs on the outside walls were filled with bricks mortared in place. This may have been to help insulate the building from the natural elements, or reduce the noise level inside from the fog signal. The

East Brother light station from the north, 1893. This is one of the earliest known photographs of the station and shows the wharf on the north side. (National Archives)

brick may also have been used to increase the mass of the building to make it more stable in high winds.

An additional contractor, E. M. Benjamin, was hired to build a cistern, rain catchment basin, wharf, tramway, boathouse, and outhouses. The lantern room, lens, and oil lamps were furnished and installed by the government. By February the lighthouse was nearly ready to send forth its first flashes. Keepers were hired, and a printed "Notice to Mariners" was distributed announcing that the light would go into operation the evening of March 1, 1874.

As the time of first lighting approached, one of the Lighthouse Service's lampists, T. L. Winship, came to the island to instruct the keepers on the fine points of lamp care and operation. The apparatus was delicate and the lighthouse authorities wanted to make sure the new keepers knew how to make the many fine adjustments that assured the flame

NOTICE TO MARINERS.

(*No. 7, of* 1874.)

UNITED STATES OF AMERICA—PACIFIC COAST CALIFORNIA.

Flashing Light and Steam Fog-Signal, on East Brother Island, off Point San Pablo, in the Straits of San Pablo, connecting San Franciso and San Pablo Bays.

Notice is hereby given that a flashing white light will be exhibited, on and after the evening of March 1, 1874, from a structure recently erected on the western end of the small island off Point San Pablo, in the Straits connecting San Francisco Bay and San Pablo Bay, and known as the East Brother.

The apparatus is of the 4th order of the system of Fresnel, and will show white flashes, at intervals of 30 seconds.

The tower is square, of wood, and is attached to the keeper's dwelling, which is also of wood.

The focal plane is 37½ feet above the base of the building, and 62½ feet above the mean level of low water.

In clear weather, the eye being elevated 15 feet above the water, the light should be seen at a distance of 13½ nautical miles.

The dome of the lantern is painted red, the remainder of the structure of a light buff color.

The geographical position of the light derived from the Coast Survey, is as follows:

Latitude, 37° 57′ 39″ North.
Longitude, 122° 26′ 01″ West.

Magnetic variation in September, 1873, 16° 24′ East.

The following are the compass bearings, and distances in nautical miles of prominent objects:

Penole Point, NE. by N. ¼ N., distant four and three-tenths miles.
Point San Pablo, N.E. ¼ E. distant three-tenths of a mile.
East tangent to Red Rock, S. by E. ¾ E., distant two miles.
West tangent to Outer Castro Rock, SE. ¾ S., distant two miles.
West tanget, Southampton Shoal, SE. by S. ½ S., distant three and five-tenths miles.
Wharf at San Quentin, SW., distant two and four-tenths miles.
The Sisters, Eastern Rock, NW. by N. ¼ N., distant one and five-tenths miles.

A 10-inch steam fog-signal is being placed on the island, at its eastern end, 150 feet from the light-house and the machinery will be contained in a small wooden building, painted the same light buff color as the light-house keeper's dwelling.

Due notice will be given of the commencement of this signal.

BY ORDER OF THE LIGHT-HOUSE BOARD:

JOSEPH HENRY,
Chairman.

TREASURY DEPARTMENT,
OFFICE LIGHT-HOUSE BOARD,
Washington, D. C., January 31, 1874.

Notice to mariners. (National Archives)

would burn steadily and at maximum brightness throughout each night. On March 1, as sunset approached, Mr. Winship, the keeper, and the two assistant keepers climbed the staircase to the top of the tower. The lampist then lighted the light for the first time, and the long-awaited beacon at last flashed its signal to passing ships.

The fog signal was also ready to operate, but there had not been enough rain to provide water for the boiler. This left the Twelfth District engineer, Lt. Col. R. S. Williamson, with a dilemma: should he postpone operation of the fog signal until the start of the next rainy season, or should fresh water be purchased and delivered to the island? Soon, however, the fog drifted in, giving him no choice but the latter. Perhaps he now had second thoughts about Molera's compressed-air trumpet! By April 9 enough water had been delivered to fire up the boiler and give the whistle a test blast. On May 1 it went into regular operation whenever there was fog.

South elevation and floor plans for East Brother lighthouse, drafted in 1872. (Modified from originals in National Archives)

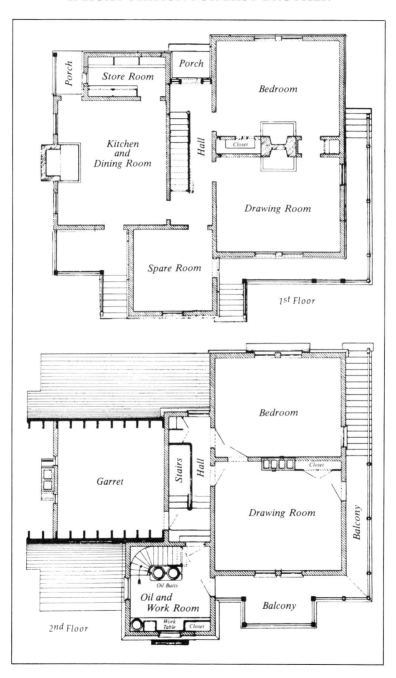

1st Floor

2nd Floor

33

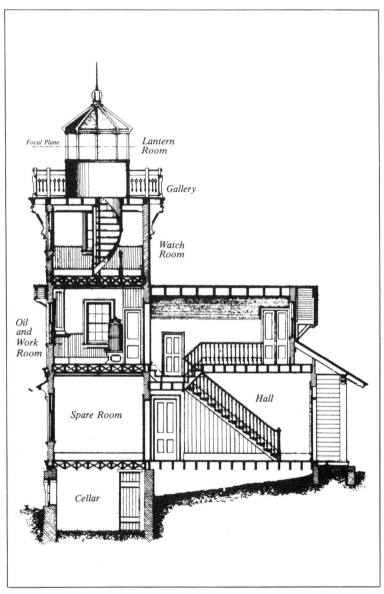

This cross section of the lighthouse was included with the architect's original drawings. Cellar below tower was omitted when the lighthouse was constructed. (Modified from original in National Archives)

Early Years at the Lighthouse

The first keeper appointed to East Brother light station was Samuel A. Farran. He served during the early years of the station with First Assistant John Cawley and Second Assistant P. Moran. Altogether eleven men served as principal keepers and twenty-five as assistant keepers (not counting substitutes) between 1874 and 1945. Some stayed only a few months, others for nearly twenty years. Not much is known of East Brother's early keepers, but surviving lighthouse records, instruction manuals, and journals paint a detailed picture of the routine of lighthouse life.

To be qualified for the job, keepers had to be able to read, write, and keep accurate records. They had to have enough physical strength and mechanical ability to maintain the buildings and equipment and make minor repairs. In the case of East Brother Island, they also had to be able to row or sail a boat to and from shore. Their foremost duties were making sure that the light operated each night between sunset and sunrise, and that the fog signal operated in times of fog.

The nightly routine began at sunset when one of the keepers would fill the lamp reservoir with special high-grade lard oil. He then used a small hand lamp to light the circular wick. The flame was positioned low at first so that the glass chimney would not crack from a quick change of temperature. It took half an hour to bring the flame up to its full height of 1-13/16 inches. On clear nights, the tiny flame could be seen a distance of 13½ nautical miles. This distance was achieved due to the powerful lens which surrounded the lamp and focused the light. The lens was actually made up of over fifty different lenses and prisms set in a brass framework. Although the flame burned continuously, the light appeared to flash because the lens focused the light into several separate beams, radiating outward horizontally like the spokes of a wheel. The lens rotated slowly on a vertical axis, powered by a clockwork mechanism. Mariners would see a flash every thirty seconds when a beam was cast in their direction.

The light was watched continuously each night, with the work divided equally among keepers. The keepers kept an eye on the light from the small room immediately below the lantern, appropriately called the watch room. Periodically, the keeper on duty cranked up the weight that powered the clockwork. He also had to wipe the glass panes of the lantern room regularly with dry towels to keep the glass free from moisture when the lens was in operation—a demanding chore in misty weather. At sunrise the wick was turned down to extinguish the light and the apparatus readied for the next night.

Keepers took special care of the delicate lens. Early each morning the lens was cleaned with a feather brush to remove dust. It was then wiped with a soft linen cloth. Finally, it was polished with a buff-skin. If oil or grease was spilled on any part of the lens it was wiped off with a linen cloth moistened with "spirits of wine." While working around the lamp and lens, keepers wore linen aprons to reduce dust and to prevent the lens from being scratched by wearing apparel and buttons. During the daytime, curtains were drawn in the lantern room to prevent discoloration of the lens by sunlight.

The type of lens then used at East Brother was called a Fresnel lens (pronounced frā-nel'), named after the French physicist Augustin Jean Fresnel. He perfected the lens design in 1822 after being commissioned by the French government to devise a method of improving the lighting apparatus in lighthouses.[11] Up to that time, parabolic reflectors, made of silvered metal, were placed behind lamps to focus the light—but with inadequate results. France quickly capitalized on Fresnel's marvelous invention and had virtually a world-wide monopoly on lighthouse lens manufacture through most of the 1800s.

Fresnel lenses were constructed in seven sizes, the largest being a first-order lens, the smallest being a sixth-order lens. (There was also a three-and-one-half-order optic.) East Brother originally had a revolving fourth-order lens, which measured about thirty-three inches high and twenty-four inches in diameter. Lenses of the fourth-order and smaller were typically used in bays and harbors where a range of ten to fourteen miles visibility on clear nights was sufficient. First-order lenses, about nine feet high and six feet in diameter, were placed in lighthouses on the open coast where more powerful lights were needed. Some of these seacoast lights were designed to have ranges of twenty-five miles or more.

Fresnel's invention makes efficient use of the light by capturing up to eighty-five percent of the light rays that radiate downward or upward from the lamp and focusing them horizontally along a single plane. The lenses are so effective that they remain in use at many lighthouses. In central California, Fresnel lenses have been in use continuously at the Point Pinos, Point Bonita, and Yerba Buena Island lighthouses since they began operation in the 1800s.

Another remarkable feature of these lenses is that they can be used to produce many different characteristics. In 1880, for example, the Lighthouse Board decided to change East Brother's light from flashing to fixed. Workmen replaced the rotating lens with a fixed fourth-order lens which produced a continuous beam of light in all directions. The board said only that "the change was desirable."

At the time of the lens change, a new lamp was installed

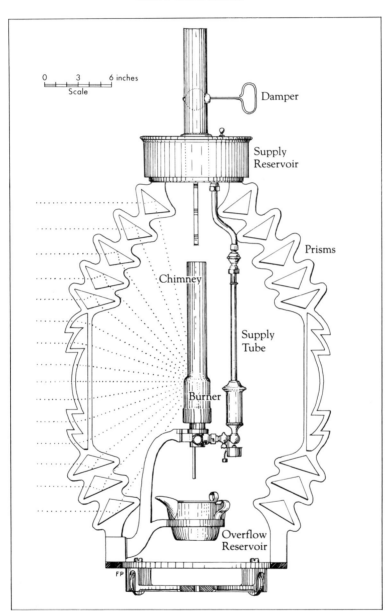

Cross section of lens showing lard oil lamp and paths of light rays. (Modified from *Instructions and Directions to Guide Light-House Keepers . . .*, Government Printing Office: 1870)

From 1880 to 1934 East Brother had a fourth-order Fresnel lens similar to this one at Yerba Buena Island. In 1983 the Coast Guard located a classical Fresnel lens for use again at East Brother. (Photo by Frank Perry)

which burned kerosene. In the late 1870s and early 1880s nearly all United States lighthouses were converted from lard oil to kerosene, then termed "mineral oil." Kerosene not only cost less than lard oil, but the kerosene lamps burned longer on a given quantity of fuel. There was considerable expense in making the change, however, since new lamps had to be supplied to each station, and new containers had to be made for storing and transporting the more volatile fuel.

Besides tending the illuminating apparatus, the keepers also maintained the fog signal, located in the building at the east end of the island. The device was a simple steam plant, similar to that of a steamboat or locomotive. It consisted of a boiler with a firebox below where coal was burned. A small pipe supplied water to the boiler from one of the station's freshwater storage tanks. Steam was used to sound the whistle, located on top of the building, and also to power a small piston engine beside the boiler. This engine regulated the timing of the whistle blasts and pumped more water into the boiler. Every twenty-four seconds a rotating cam in the engine alternately triggered blasts of four and eight seconds. Mariners could check the latest issue of the *Light List* to identify the station from the characteristic of either the light or the fog signal.*

The whistle was sometimes more important in aiding mariners than the light. In dense fog or heavy rain East Brother's powerful light was virtually useless. The ten-inch whistle, on the other hand, could often be heard from ten or twelve miles away. Through the years many a ship captain groped his way across the misty bay waters guided only by the regular blasts of East Brother's fog signal. It took many years' experience to learn to navigate in this way. Echoes off the surrounding hills could easily deceive the inexperienced ear as to the true direction of the signal.

Steam whistles were used at many United States fog signal stations in the late nineteenth and early twentieth centuries. However, they had some significant disadvantages. The engine needed constant oiling and tinkering, and often major replacement parts. Since the whistle might be put in operation night or day, off-duty keepers had to learn to sleep in spite of the noise. Some keepers apparently got quite good at this. The instruction manual supplied to keepers in 1881 stated explicitly: "Whenever the apparatus is in operation, a keeper must be in the engine-house, in charge, and awake."

It took about forty-five minutes to build up enough steam in the boiler to put the signal in operation. To compensate for this delay, a large bell was installed on East Brother in

*The *Light List*, published annually by the government since the mid 1800s, lists lighthouses and other navigational aids.

Early view of fog signal building. Steam whistle is immediately to left of large smokestack. (Courtesy Nels Stenmark)

April, 1878. If the fog came in suddenly, one of the keepers or a family member would strike the bell at fifteen-second intervals until the whistle could be sounded. When the signal was not in use, the firebox was kept loaded with coal, ready for lighting at a moment's notice. Deciding when to start the fog signal required much more judgment on the part of the keeper than when to light the lamp. Sometimes when fog started to come in, the boilers would be fired up, only to have the fog go out again. In general, when Red Rock, Point San Quentin, or The Sisters became obscured by bad weather, it was time to fire up the boiler.

Coal was used both as fuel for the fog signal boiler and for domestic use. In the latter case wood was also used. Several times each year one of the lighthouse tenders such as the *Shubrick, Madroño,* or *Manzanita* would deliver a supply of

Boiler and fireboxes inside the fog signal building. (U.S. Coast Guard)

This timing device beside the boiler regulated the whistle blasts. (U.S. Coast Guard)

coal to the station wharf. The keepers had to haul the ninety-pound sacks of coal up a tramway on a rail car then place them in the coal shed. The tenders often unloaded eight or ten tons, and sometimes even thirty or forty tons of coal at one time. Not surprisingly, keepers spent a good deal of time hauling coal. During fiscal 1900-1901 the signal alone consumed about forty tons—enough to operate some 252 hours that year. Actually, that was modest compared to other central California fog signals. Those at Point Montara, Point Bonita, and Point Reyes, often blasted away for over 1,000 hours per year.

The wharf at East Brother, originally located on the north side of the island, became a regular source of frustration. In the spring of 1875, only a year after the station began functioning, the wharf and tramway were badly damaged by heavy waves during a gale. According to keeper Farran, the "sea broke over the island."[12] Temporary repairs were made, and the following September more piles were driven. These were bound together with twelve-inch-square timbers. The wharf was also raised three feet, prompting the Lighthouse Board to boast that it was now "so strengthened as to withstand any ordinary storm."[13]

Apparently the storm of early 1880 was not ordinary. The wharf suffered major damage. Again it was repaired and lasted another five years until February 10, 1885. That morning the crew of the lighthouse tender *Manzanita* planned to unload fifteen tons of coal for the station. They unloaded ten tons when suddenly the section of wharf supporting the coal gave way, dumping the coal into the bay. The soggy sacks of coal had to be retrieved at low tide. Later in the month a crew of carpenters repaired the damage.

In 1894 the wharf was declared unsafe—this time before it had a chance to collapse. The culprits were teredos—worm-like marine mollusks which bore into wood. A new wharf was built, sixty feet long and twenty feet wide, this time supported by paraffin-coated steel-shod piles driven ten feet into the rock bottom.

Despite the romantic portrayal of lighthouse keeping in novels, poems, and art, the job was monotonous and the Lighthouse Board knew it. Pay was modest and much of the work boring. Nevertheless, the board did its best within budget to provide adequate accommodations and conveniences for keepers. It hoped to attract men of high caliber into the service and encourage them to stay.

In 1874 the keeper at East Brother earned $800 per year—paid quarterly. The first assistant earned $600, the second assistant $550. Actually this was reasonable pay at the time, especially considering that the job came with a place to live. However, salaries were not increased for nearly forty years.

For the intellectual benefit of keepers, the Lighthouse Board in the 1880s assembled portable lending libraries which circulated from station to station. Each came in its

Lighthouse tender *Madroño*. Photo taken from East Brother, early 1900s. (U.S. Coast Guard)

own combination bookcase and shipping crate and contained about fifty books. Included were novels, poetry, books on history and science, a Bible, and a prayer book. After several months, the library could be exchanged for another when the lighthouse tender came.

During the 1870s the keepers and their families at East Brother were provided with rations. These were delivered periodically by tender as was standard practice at many remote stations. In 1880 the Lighthouse Board decided East Brother was not sufficiently remote to warrant continuing this service. The keepers then had to row or sail to Point San Quentin or Point San Pedro to do marketing. This may have been for the best. The annual allowance per man for 1881 was:

Pork	200 pounds
Beef	100 pounds
Flour	2 barrels
Rice	50 pounds
Brown sugar	50 pounds
Coffee (green grain)	24 pounds
Beans or peas	10 gallons
Vinegar	4 gallons
Potatoes	2 barrels

Not exactly the makings of a gourmet dinner! Keepers were instructed that the quantities could be changed, so long as the total cost of the rations was not thereby made greater. In the 1890s and early 1900s rations were again supplied to the island residents by the government, mostly as a supplement comprised of potatoes and onions.

Keepers had to be jacks-of-all-trades. Besides tending the light and steam whistle, they also cleaned the cistern and rainshed; repaired fences, windows and minor storm damage; built cupboards and tables as needed; and kept the boats in good repair. There was also painting—always painting—whether it was painting the tower, lantern room, fog signal building, boat, boathouse, their living quarters, or whatever. Many of the keepers liked to paint. Things always looked so much better with a fresh coat of paint, and applying it required neither great physical strain nor too much thought. In fact, by 1894 keepers at East Brother and other Twelfth District stations were apparently doing *too much* painting. Inspector Henry Nichols, annoyed by the ". . .excessive unnecessary use of paint at some stations," ordered that henceforth no painting of any kind be done without his prior approval.[14] At least for awhile after that, keepers had to make written requests for paint including a statement of the work to be done, the amount of paint on hand, the estimated quantity of paint needed, and when the job was last done.

Such thrift was typical of the Lighthouse Service. Nothing was wasted. The coal sacks, once emptied, were rolled up and returned to the tender for reuse. Oil cans and other containers were likewise used over and over. Before a new tool or container would be issued to a keeper, the old one had to be turned in, otherwise its cost would be deducted from his salary.

The keepers at East Brother were given a manual of instructions which told in great detail everything they needed to know to run the station. It included diagrams of the lamp and fog signal with all the parts labeled. It covered instructions for mixing paint, cleaning brushes, and a recipe for whitewash. Lest they have any doubt when the lamp was to be lighted or extinguished, they were provided with a booklet of tables showing the exact times of sunset and sunrise for each day of the year.

The principal keeper had the added chore of keeping records. Each month he submitted a report on the condition of the station to both the inspector and engineer; he also had to turn in a fog signal report and an absence report. Quarterly, he accounted for expenditures of oil and submitted vouchers for salaries. When necessary, the keeper filed returns for receipt of supplies delivered, any damage to the station, any unusual occurrence, and a shipwreck report. The keeper also maintained a daily expenditure book, a general accounting book, and a daily journal of events at the station.

The keepers' workload increased even more in the 1890s when several other government agencies requested assistance from the Lighthouse Service. The Census Bureau asked that keepers send in reports on fish and fishing observed in the area of their station. Soon keepers were also asked to file reports on earthquakes and to record rainfall.

Besides the routine jobs, the men also had to be prepared for the unexpected. They kept a close watch for vessels in distress and several times rescued people from boats that capsized. When storms hit, East Brother's residents often had problems of their own. On a number of occasions one of the station's two boats was torn from its mooring and damaged or destroyed. Indeed there were times when nobody could get on or off the island because of rough water. On April 1, 1892, Keeper P. J. Quinlan left on what was intended to be a one day trip to San Francisco. However, high winds and rough waters prevented his return for three days. On another occasion the same keeper returned to the island at 11:30 at night only to find the light out! The assistant, Martin Haave, had left the station in the other boat and capsized. He managed to stay afloat, but could not return to the lighthouse in time to light the lamp. This excuse must have satisfied the inspector, for the assistant stayed on for three more years.

Throughout East Brother's early history there were no major shipwrecks in the area—a tribute both to the men who designed and built the station's equipment and to the keepers who so carefully maintained it.

The S.S. *Arrow* ferry passing East Brother, circa 1904. (National Maritime Museum, San Francisco)

Pages from the Past

The bound journals kept by the successive keepers at East Brother light station chronicle over seventy years of daily life on the island. For the most part, keepers confined each day's entry to a single line, usually describing the weather and the day's work, but on some occasions elaborating. In reading the hand-written entries across the yellowing pages, one develops a sense of what it was like to live and work at this light station. A surprising amount of information lies in these pages: the accounts of ships in distress; the reports of the endless cleaning, repairing, and painting; the inspections; the arrival of coal and supplies; and the regular trips across the bay for mail and food. One wonders if the keepers ever considered that someone might read all this a hundred years later. We will never know.

In 1882 Charles F. Winsor was keeper; Joseph Page was first assistant. There are many clues in Winsor's writings about him and his assistant and how they lived. Some of the entries answer questions, others raise them. Many are redundant, but others unusual. Imagine it is July, 1883, and that you are the inspector for the Twelfth Lighthouse District. Examine the journal entries for the past fiscal year and see what you can learn about East Brother light station and the men on duty there:

July 1, 1882: Wind S.W., strong. Cleaned up the engine and about the house.

July 2: Wind S.W., strong. Sunday.

July 5: Wind S.W., light. Mr. Page took quarterly, monthly

49

and annual returns to San Quentin. Laid platform on tank.

July 8: Wind S., light, smoky and hazy. General cleaning and washing, etc., etc.

July 10: Wind S., strong, smoky and hazy. But little done.

July 14: Wind S.W., strong. Mr. Page left for San Quentin A.M., capsized off the buoy near the West Brother at 12:15 P.M. Capt. Winsor hailed the Steamer *Reform* passing up at the time and sent her to his relief. The *Reform* picked him up ¼ of a mile N.N.E. of the Light House and landed him and the boat at the dock at 1:15 P.M. Oars, rudder, mail and all the marketing consisting of mutton, cabbages, peas, etc., etc., lost, also milk and can.

July 15: Wind S.W., strong. Fitted rudder temporarily to boat.

August 9: Wind S.W., strong and hazy. *Manzanita* came at 10:45 A.M. Comd. Coffin and Capt. Payson landed then proceeded to Mare Island to attend the funeral of Rear Admiral McDougal.*

August 14: Wind S.W., strong, cloudy and hazy. Mr. Page repairing sail to boat. L.H. depot boat 76 landed yearly supplies and 6 sacks coal/soft.

August 16: Wind S.W., strong, cloudy and hazy. Mr. Page to Pt. Pablo for drift[wood] on the beach.

August 21: Wind S.W., strong, hazy. Painted rail around top of tower.

August 22: Wind S.W., strong, hazy. Cleaned engine and oiled same, also pump.

August 23: Wind S.W., strong, hazy. Mr. Page went for vegetables and butter to Point Pedro.

August 24: Wind S.W., strong, hazy. Building tables and bunks. Repaired drill.

September 4: Wind S.S.W., smoky and hazy. Waiting for Engineers—Mr. Shaw and 3 men at 2 P.M.

*David McDougal, former commandant at Mare Island.

September 5: Wind S.S.W., light, smoky and hazy. At work on watershed.* Mr. Page gone to San Quentin for a week.

September 6: Wind S.S.W., smoky and hazy. Sch. *Cecilia Maria* arrived with 40 tons gravel at 2 P.M.

September 12: Wind S.S.W., foggy at 4 A.M. 'till 10 A.M. Men at work on shed. Mr. Page picked up a shift.

September 28: Wind S.W., light, smoky and hazy. Finished watershed and commenced on dome of tank. *Manzanita* anchored [off] W. Brother.

October 4: Wind N.E., clear. Mr. Page went to San Quentin for Mr. Smith to serve as assistant during his absence.

October 9: Wind N.E., cloudy. Mr. Smith went for boatload of soil Pt. Pablo. Finished steps and repaired fence.

October 11: Wind N.W., clear. Repairing fence and railway track.

October 15: Wind N.W., clear. Sunday. Beautiful day.

October 31: Wind N.W., light, later part strong. *Manzanita* passed at 9 A.M. and anchored off the sisters to buoy a sunken wreck.

December 14: Wind N.E. Foggy from 4 A.M. to 10 A.M. Mr. Page went to San Quentin for mail, returned as usual, drunk.

December 16: Wind N.E., light. Foggy from 5:50 A.M. to 12 noon. Fog very dense 'till 11 A.M. Cleaned boiler at noon. A large four masted ship ashore about 1/3 dist. from Point Pedro to Marin Islands. Two tugs took her off at 4 o'clock P.M. and proceeded towards S. Francisco.

December 20: Wind N.E., clear. Painted over water spouts around the house. Comd. Coffin and Captain Payson, L.H. Engineer, landed at 10 o'clock P.M. and made an inspection.

January 2, 1883: Wind S., light, hazy. Mr. Page took the mail over to San Quentin, returned drunk.

January 11: Wind N.E., cold, light, foggy. Mr. Page went for

*A concrete rainshed was built to replace the original asphalt shed.

the mail, returned at 2:30 P.M., drunk, mail wet.

January 19: Wind N.N.E., commenced blowing at 2 o'clock A.M. Noon, blowing a gale and a heavy sea running over the wharf at 3 P.M.; washed away the lower portion of steps.

January 22: Wind N.N.E., fresh, very smoky all day. Cold, 40°.

February 7: Wind N.E., light, foggy. *Manzanita* landed at noon 6 tons H, 4 tons S coal.

February 8: Wind N.E., light, clear. Mr. Page went for mail and stores, drunk, no mail.

February 9: Wind N.E., light, clear. Hauled up the hard coal and stored it away, also the wood, 1 cord.

February 10: Wind N.E., light, clear. Mr. Albert Tippett entered on his duties as assistant (1st) at this station.

February 14: Wind S.W., squally, strong. Employed all day cleaning engine room and lens in lantern.

Early view of the lighthouse. (Courtesy Nels Stenmark)

February 21: Wind N.E., light, clear. Painted lantern and floor, front-hall stairs, back porch and front porch.

March 10: Wind S., light, foggy. Kept fires banked 'till 12:30.

April 8: Wind N.W., strong, clear. Sunday. Cleaning and washing lens in tower, badly smoked.

April 12: Wind N.W., strong, squally. Mr. Tippett started for San Quentin and put back, *too rough.*

April 13: Wind N.E., clear. Between 8 and 9 o'clock P.M. a steamer passed by and sounded three whistles. As no answer was sounded from the bell, I call to Mr. Tippett to reply. But he was not satisfied that the whistle was for the station and the boat was so far away by the time I could satisfy him by explaining, she was beyond hearing.

May 29: Wind S.W., strong, hazy. Mr. Tippett went to S. Quentin to consult the doctor.

June 2: Wind S.W., strong. *Manzanita* landed supplies for year coming July, 1883. Inspector on board. Delivered Library No. 35.

June 6: Wind N.E., light, clear. Thermometer 95° in the shade.

The Stenmark Era

The register of keepers at East Brother kept during the late 1800s reveals that well over half were European immigrants. There were natives of Denmark, Sweden, Norway, England, and several from Ireland. John O. Stenmark, who was appointed keeper in 1894, was a native of Sweden and was assisted at the station until 1901 by another Swedish immigrant, James Anderson. Thanks to old newspaper clippings, photos, and other records kept by Stenmark children and grandchildren, more is known about him than about most of the East Brother keepers.

Stenmark was born in 1865 and emigrated to the United States at age twenty. In 1888 he joined the U.S. Lighthouse Service. His first job was working as a crewman aboard the lighthouse tender *Madroño*. At that time equipment and supplies for most lighthouses were delivered by ship. The 180-foot-long *Madroño* had a crew of nineteen and steamed about 10,000 miles each year servicing lighthouses and buoys throughout California. The lighthouse inspector was usually on board to deliver the keepers' pay and to inspect the station. It was while Stenmark was helping unload supplies for the Point Conception lighthouse that he saved the life of Inspector Thomas Perry.

Point Conception stands out as the most pronounced point along the California coast. Consequently, seas there can be particularly rough. Stenmark and some of his fellow crew members were trying to get a small boatload of supplies to shore from the tender. Suddenly, a rough wave capsized the

John Stenmark served as keeper at East Brother for nearly twenty years. (Courtesy Nels Stenmark)

boat, dumping the men and supplies into the water. Perry was carried helplessly away by the heavy seas and was soon in serious trouble. The other crew members clung fearfully to the capsized boat as young Stenmark, bleeding from a cut on his head caused by a breaking oar, swam towards the inspector. Just as the inspector was about to go under, Stenmark reached him and struggled unsuccessfully to swim to shore, holding the officer's head above water. Both men nearly drowned before finally being rescued by the tender.[15]

John Stenmark was highly commended for his bravery. As a reward, on August 1, 1890, he was appointed assistant keeper at Año Nuevo Island fog signal station. Located forty-five miles south of San Francisco, the island supported a twelve-inch steam fog whistle and a small lens-lantern for a light. Although an improvement over life on the lighthouse tender, conditions on the tiny island were far from ideal. Stenmark and his wife, Breta, shared with the principal keeper a tiny cottage that had been partitioned into two living areas. The island residents could only get to and from the island by rowboat. Navigating through the surf, while trying to avoid the rocks around Año Nuevo Point, always made crossing the half-mile channel dangerous. In 1883 four men, including the keeper and assistant, drowned while trying to make the crossing.[16]

Stenmark must have been an able assistant, for in 1892, when keeper Henry Hall was transferred, Stenmark was appointed keeper at Año Nuevo. He continued helping others, several times rescuing fishermen whose boats capsized near the island. In 1894 the Stenmarks' first daughter, Annie, was born at Año Nuevo. Three months later John Stenmark was transferred to East Brother and the young family set up housekeeping on San Francisco Bay. The island was smaller, but the house was bigger, and bay waters usually calmer. The Stenmarks quickly grew to like their new home and stayed almost twenty years.

Mr. and Mrs. Stenmark made the most of the small piece of land. They brought soil from the mainland and grew vegetables in a tiny garden in front of the lighthouse. In pens they raised goats, pigs, rabbits, and chickens. During his first few years as keeper, Stenmark, like his predecessors, rowed the 2½ miles to Point San Quentin to do shopping and get mail. Prior to the birth of each of his two sons he rowed all the way to San Quentin and back to fetch the doctor.

The Stenmarks had four children: Annie, Ruby, Phillip, and Folke. For several years when the children were young the government paid for a teacher to live at East Brother part of each year and tutor the children. Later, when a road was built from Point San Pablo to the town of Point Richmond, the children attended school there. By that time, mail and provisions were picked up at Point Richmond instead of Point San Quentin.

Daughter Annie lived for the first twenty years of her life on the island until she met and married Charles Morisette. Morisette worked a short distance from the lighthouse at the Standard Oil refinery. "My hubby, Charlie, used to come

The Stenmarks often entertained friends and relatives on the island as shown in these old photos from their family album. (Courtesy Nels Stenmark)

courting to the island," she recalled fondly in later years. "He couldn't row very good at first, but we soon taught him."[17] When the couple got married in June, 1914, the newspaper announced "Cupid Ends Lighthouse Romance":

> A romance that had its beginning beneath the tall, gray tower of the Brothers Lighthouse, located [off] Point Orient, culminated in a happy marriage at Oakland yesterday when Charles Morisette, a foreman at the Standard Oil wharf, claimed Miss Annie E. Stenmark as his bride.
>
> Miss Stenmark is the daughter of John O. Stenmark, lighthouse keeper [off] that point, and it was while assisting her father about his duties of caring for the great white light that flashes across the treacherous waters of the upper San Pablo bay that she became acquainted with Morisette.[18]

Despite living on an island, the Stenmarks had many friends in the surrounding bay area. They sometimes entertained as many as fifty friends and relatives at the lighthouse. On the occasion of their nineteenth wedding anniversary, the local newspaper described the gathering:

> The guests were carried across to the light house from Bailey's wharf in row boats, and as the bay was calm everyone enjoyed the trip immensely.
>
> The rooms were very prettily decorated for the occasion and the evening was spent with music and dancing. Dainty refreshments were served at the proper time, after which hearty congratulations and best wishes were extended to the host and hostess.[19]

John Stenmark retired as keeper of East Brother in July, 1914. The family moved to Richmond, where they owned and operated the Stenmark Hotel on Fifteenth Street. Stenmark died only a year later in 1915 while on board the steamer, *City of Topeka,* traveling up the coast from San Francisco.

East Brother light station benefited from numerous improvements during the two decades Stenmark served as keeper. The lighthouse and fog signal gained renewed importance following construction of the Standard Oil refinery in Richmond in 1901. Docks for tankers were built along the San Pablo shoreline only a few hundred yards from the station. In 1909 the California Wine Association also established its huge aging and bottling plant just south of Point San Pablo. The plant had a storage capacity of 12 million gallons and a 1,800-foot wharf where grapes were unloaded and barrels of wine shipped out.[20] With these and other developments, the town of Richmond ballooned in population from 200 in 1901 to 23,000 by 1917.[21]

One of the first improvements to East Brother during this era was erection of a 25,000-gallon freshwater storage tank in April, 1896. Later, two more tanks were built: a 20,000-gallon tank in 1903 and an 8,000-gallon tank in 1910. Using the steam engine from the fog signal, and an array of pipes, Stenmark could pump water from the cistern up into the tanks or vice versa. This was particularly helpful in September when he had to drain the cistern for annual cleaning.

Rainwater was not only collected from the concrete rainshed in the middle of the island, but also from the roofs

Mariner's view of East Brother, about 1908. (National Archives)

John Stenmark (right) and friend at the top of the wharf tramway. (Courtesy Nels Stenmark)

of all the buildings. The system was (and is) extremely effective, capturing 5,000 gallons from a single inch of rain. Coming from the sky, the water should have been pure and clean. At that time, however, the roofs of the buildings at East Brother and other light stations were painted with red lead paint. This prompted the Lighthouse Board to include the following caution in its *Instructions to Light-Keepers:*

> Water contaminated with chloride of lead . . . does not lose its poisonous qualities either by boiling or by exposure to the air.
>
> To purify this water, and render it perfectly fit for all culinary and domestic purposes, it will only be necessary to put some powdered chalk or whiting into each cistern in which such rain water is collected, and to stir it up well, occasionally, after rain has fallen.[22]

In July of 1903 a new wharf was built since the existing wharf had again become unstable. Instead of tearing down the wharf on the island's north side, it was simply abandoned and a new wharf was built on the east side of the island where the landing is located today. The new wharf included a derrick, boathouse, two staircases down to the water, and a tramway up to the island. This location enabled use of a steam-powered winch in the fog signal building to haul up shipments of coal and other supplies from the dock.

The new winch was soon put to good use. In February and March, 1906, workmen built a new concrete rainshed to replace the one laid in 1882. It was a huge task. Tons and tons of sand, gravel, and cement had to be hauled to the island by ship, unloaded onto the wharf, and winched up the tramway on a small railcar. The rainshed took a month to complete, but when it was finished Stenmark concluded it was the "best cement job ever laid."[23]

Less than a month later the new concrete work and all the island structures were tested by the most infamous earthquake in California history. On April 18 John Stenmark wrote in the journal: "A heavy earthquake this morning at 5:15 A.M.. Lenses of the light broken and glassware broke and everything of glass broke. Doors open of themselves and the whole island rocking. All the lenses broke." There were no reports of significant structural damage to the station but extensive repairs had to be made to the Fresnel lens. Over the next two days the Stenmarks gazed across the bay as fire consumed San Francisco. During the day billows of black smoke rose from the southern sky. At night the sky turned orange as the flames devoured block after block. "S.F. burning fearfully at 9 P.M.," Stenmark wrote on the evening of April 19. The following night he and the others on the island could see the fire move toward Black Point.

A little over a year later the station was again shaken, this time by a ship. At half past two o'clock on the morning of June 13, 1907, the steamer *A. C. Freese* approached the quarter-mile-wide channel east of the lighthouse. It came from the north, towing another steamer, the *Leader*, and two barges. As the *A. C. Freese* steamed through the channel the *Leader* was caught by the currents, drifted toward the island, and struck the wharf. The steamer knocked the entire wharf askew, snapping piles, and knocking the boathouse off its foundation. On impact the two five-inch tow ropes snapped like pieces of string. Stenmark, hearing the collision, raced down to the wharf and boarded the vessel. The only crewman on board admitted that he and the man on one of the barges had been asleep when the boat struck. The frustrated keeper was unable to find out the man's name, but recorded the names of the boats. They were owned by the California Navigation and Improvement Company of San Francisco which was eventually held responsible. In July the Thompson Bridge Company was hired to build a new wharf at a cost of $1,600.

At the time of the *Leader* collision several more improvements were being made on the island. To reduce the danger

Damage to wharf after being struck by the steamer *Leader*.
(U.S. Coast Guard)

of fire, a small oilhouse was built to store kerosene. It was
constructed of concrete and located just east of the storage
building. A new walkway was also constructed to the signal
building.

Late the following year the lighthouse was extensively
remodeled. A crew of workmen spent three months painting,
plastering, fixing gutters, replacing part of the foundation,
and raising the roof of the room over the kitchen. The inside
stairway was removed to create an additional room for the
assistant keeper, and the outside stairway was relocated to
the front of the lighthouse.

Ever since the lighthouse first cast its rays upon San
Francisco and San Pablo bays, the light had come from oil
wick lamps, first burning lard oil and then kerosene. In
June, 1912, the wick lamp at East Brother was replaced by an
incandescent oil vapor lamp (abbreviated I.O.V.). This lamp
was also fueled by kerosene, but the kerosene was forced

under pressure into a vapor chamber. There it vaporized and passed upward to the mantle where it was ignited, burning as a brilliant ball of glowing gas. It worked much like the Coleman lamps used today by campers.

An I.O.V. lamp was first introduced at a lighthouse in France in 1898.[24] The first installation at a U.S. lighthouse was in New Jersey in 1904. Proving to be much more powerful than wick lamps, this type of lamp was soon installed at most of the important United States lighthouses. By 1912 East Brother was one of twenty-seven lighthouses in California utilizing the new device.

When the new lamp was installed the characteristic of the light was changed from fixed to occulting so that it would less likely be confused with lights on shore. The light was termed occulting rather than flashing because the period of light was longer than the period of dark—in this case, light, 7½ seconds; dark, 2½ seconds. To produce the new characteristic yet avoid the high cost of a new lens, lighthouse engineers cleverly modified the old lens by replacing one of its four lens panels with an opaque screen and remounting the lens so that it would rotate on its axis. A clockwork mechanism similar to that used earlier in the station's history powered the lens, rotating it once every ten seconds. The screen blocked out the light for a quarter of the ten-second rotation.

The new lamp and lens combination produced a light rated at 2,900 candlepower as compared to only 520 candlepower before. Another benefit of the I.O.V. lamp was that it used less fuel. The only disadvantage was that it was often temperamental. After the lamp was installed, it took Keeper Stenmark several days to get it to function properly. After that it still seemed that some part of the apparatus had to be fixed nearly once a week.

Mrs. Stenmark poses beside bell which was struck by hand every fifteen seconds until there was sufficient steam pressure to run the fog whistle. This could take forty-five minutes. In 1907 this chore was eliminated when a mechanical striking apparatus was installed. (Stenmark collection, Richmond City Museum)

Keeper John P. Kofod painting the side of the dwelling. (Courtesy Walter Fanning)

Later Years at East Brother

In 1910 the Lighthouse Board was replaced by the Bureau of Lighthouses which was under the U.S. Commerce Department. Back in 1852, at the time the Lighthouse Board was created, America's lighthouse system was of a size that allowed improvement and management by a committee of men of diverse backgrounds. By 1910, however, the agency had grown so large that the committee approach was abandoned in favor of an administration headed by a single individual. For most of its twenty-nine-year existence the bureau was headed by George Putnam, Commissioner of Lighthouses. Putnam was a civilian, had worked for the Coast Survey, and was a skilled administrator.

The Bureau of Lighthouses was entirely a civilian agency and operated that way until 1939, when its duties were transferred to the U.S. Coast Guard. When the bureau was formed, some of the men who had risen through the ranks as assistants and keepers were promoted to inspectors. They replaced the naval officers who had supervised each lighthouse district under the Lighthouse Board. Civilian engineers, draftsmen, and mechanics were also employed. The Lighthouse Service now relied more than ever on men who had decided to make the service a career. One such man was John P. Kofod.

John Kofod became keeper at East Brother July 25, 1914. He had joined the Lighthouse Service in 1899 as third assistant keeper at Point Sur. He then served at Point Reyes and later moved to Yerba Buena Island. With the transfer to

Keeper John P. Kofod with his wife, Metha, and grandchildren, Walter and Erma Fanning, 1918. (Courtesy Walter Fanning)

East Brother came a promotion to keeper. Kofod and his wife made the move to East Brother with their furniture and belongings on board the lighthouse tender *Madroño*.

Kofod was born in Copenhagen, Denmark, in the early 1860s and came to the United States as a young man. After arriving in New York, he took a ship to Panama, traveled across the isthmus by railroad, and then sailed up the West Coast to San Francisco. There he met Metha Jorgensen, also a Danish immigrant, whom he married in 1886. Kofod worked as a glazier, specializing in stained-glass windows for churches. It was during a slump in this trade that he decided to join the Lighthouse Service.

Walter Fanning, grandson of John and Metha Kofod, remembers well his visits to the island as a child during and just after World War I. He recalls that, during the war, victory gardens were promoted just as in World War II. "My grandfather hauled soil in five-gallon kerosene tins from the mainland to the island, forming beds between the watershed and the outer fence. He couldn't use the scarce fresh water so he carried bath and wash water to his vegetables."[25] The Kofods also raised chickens which they kept in pens outside the main fence at the island's west end.

The keeper liked to go fishing and, of course, did not have far to go. "Striped bass were caught on lures drifted from the wharf on the incoming tide and by trolling from boats," recalls his grandson. The excess bass caught each fall was salted down in wooden casks, providing almost a year-round supply. From the station wharf young Fanning liked to catch rock cod and perch. These his grandmother would cook for dinner.

Fanning also recalls the heavy ship traffic at that time:

> The Monticello line between Vallejo and San Francisco passed each way just about hourly. The *Delta Queen* and the *Delta King* made a trip a day, and there were many stern-wheeled freight carriers.
>
> Dozens of scow-schooners carried hay and grain from the central valleys to the bay cities. The collision between the Monticello steamers *Sehome* and *General Frisbie* just north of the island in December, 1918, was a memorable event. The *Sehome* sank, and a deck house drifted down to the island and was made fast in the little cove on the west side. It broke away before anything could be done with it.

As children Walter Fanning and his sister liked to go into the fog signal building, particularly on cold days. "It was warm from the two boiler furnaces and smelled pleasantly of steam and hot oil." Their grandfather or the assistant kept close watch over the gauges, shoveling in coal when the

John and Metha Kofod beside century plant, West Brother in the distance. (Courtesy Walter Fanning)

John and Metha Kofod on left, with the assistant and his wife. The dog's name is Teddy. (Courtesy Walter Fanning)

pressure dropped, raking out coal if the pressure grew too high. The coal was piled in the north room of the signal building beside the winch and tram car. There was also a well-equipped tool room in the building with tools neatly mounted on wall brackets. "They were beautifully maintained and never used," says Fanning. "My grandfather had tools of his own."

John Kofod moonlighted for a short time during the war, working in the Standard Oil Refinery a few days each week. The government permitted keepers to have a spare-time job so long as it did not interfere with their lighthouse work. Kofod was transferred to Yerba Buena Island as keeper in 1921. He retired from the Lighthouse Service in 1929.

In 1922 Willard Miller was appointed keeper at East Brother. He served on the island for over nineteen years—nearly as long as John Stenmark. He was a quiet, modest man whose calm demeanor belied the daring experiences of his younger years.

The story of Miller's background comes mostly from Jack Lewis, nephew of Earl Snodgrass (Assistant Keeper, 1936–1943). Mr. Lewis helped his uncle and the keeper with chores around the light station as a young man and knew both men well.

Willard Miller was born in Nova Scotia in 1877 and was the son of a shipbuilder. When he was only fourteen, he stowed away on one of his father's ships. He was at sea for quite some time, was shipwrecked, and had to survive on an island for several weeks until rescued.

Miller joined the U.S. Navy in 1898 and was sent to Cuba to fight in the Spanish-American War. He was placed in command of a crew aboard a small steam launch dispatched from the U.S.S. *Nashville*. Their assignment was to cut a marine telegraph cable at the port of Cienfuegos, Cuba. He displayed extraordinary bravery and coolness throughout the mission, despite heavy fire from shore batteries. The following year he was awarded the congressional Medal of Honor for his bravery. The keeper was not one to brag, as revealed by Jack Lewis's recollections many years later. "I stumbled onto the fact that he held the medal and the deed behind it by accident, and I had to wring the story out of him."[26]

Miller left the Navy in December, 1908, and joined the Lighthouse Service the following year. Before coming to East Brother he served at the Los Angeles Harbor lighthouse located at the end of the San Pedro breakwater, and later at Roe Island in Suisun Bay.

For the first dozen years that Keeper Willard Miller was in charge of East Brother, the station operated much as before. The keeper and his assistant kept the oil vapor lamp burning each night from sunset to sunrise and fired up the steam whistle when the fog came in. As an economy measure, use of the steam whistle was discontinued annually from April 1 to September 30 beginning in 1925 (there being little fog during those months). When fog did occur during this period, the bell was rung automatically every fifteen seconds with a hammer powered by clockwork.

The most significant changes at East Brother while Willard Miller was keeper came in 1934 with electrification. In March of that year electricians arrived to wire the lighthouse for both domestic and navigational lighting. Over the next four months crews of workmen installed a new light and lens, replaced the steam fog signal with a diaphone, laid a concrete floor in the fog signal building, and installed an underwater electric cable between the island and Point San Pablo.

During the 1920s and 1930s all but the most remote of this nation's lighthouses were converted to electricity. At East Brother the rotating fourth-order lens and I.O.V. lamp were replaced by a fifth-order fixed lens with a 500-watt light bulb. The new outfit was rated at 13,000 candlepower. An

From left to right: Keeper Willard Miller, Sea Scout Jack Lewis, and First Assistant Earl Snodgrass in front of the lighthouse, late 1930s. (Courtesy Jack Lewis)

electric timer turned the light on and off, producing two flashes of two-second duration every ten seconds. The device substantially reduced the keepers' nightly chore. Though few people probably realized it at the time, this was a major turning point in the station's history and one that would someday lead to complete automation.

The diaphone fog signal was put into commission June 20, 1934. A Canadian invention, the diaphone was first introduced in the United States in 1915 and by the 1930s had come into widespread use here. The two-tone sound was produced by compressed air operating a reciprocating piston. It was superior to the steam whistle in that it was less likely to be mistaken for a ship's whistle. Another advantage was that it only took a few minutes to build up sufficient air pressure to operate. Keepers, of course, liked it because they did not have to shovel coal.

John S. Conway, in his 1923 book *The United States*

Lighthouse Service, described the diaphone sound as ending "with an abrupt roar." Lighthouse Commissioner George Putnam described it as ending with a "distinctive grunt." Visitors to East Brother today can make up their own mind how best to describe it. Everyone agrees on one thing, however: it is loud! Large diaphones have reportedly been heard a distance of twenty-five miles, though their normal range is four or five.

The diaphone at East Brother was originally installed with an electric motor to power the air compressor. A timing device triggered three-second blasts every twenty seconds. In case of a power failure, the compressor could be operated with a backup gasoline engine. If the diaphone itself malfunctioned, an electric oscillator was sounded. Both the light and the oscillator could be run by a gasoline-powered electrical generator in the fog signal building. In later years the oscillator was replaced by a duplicate diaphone to be used in the event of breakdown.

The backup systems usually had to be put to use several times each year. Ships sometimes dragged their anchors through the east channel, damaging or severing the power cable. When Miller spotted a ship doing this, he would shout warnings from the station wharf. On several occasions the cable was disconnected while the channel was dredged. One night while the cable was disconnected, the backup generator failed. Miller had to quickly place an emergency gasoline lamp in the lens.

During the last six years Willard Miller was keeper, he was assisted by Earl Snodgrass. Earl and his wife, Lillian, moved to East Brother in November, 1936. Like the keeper, the new assistant came to the job with many years' seafaring experience. He served in the Navy during World War I and afterwards worked on a tug hauling logs in Tillamook Bay, Oregon. He eventually saved up enough money to buy his own boat, the *Rustler.* He made his living with the *Rustler* by

Earl Snodgrass on dome of cistern. Note diaphone atop roof of signal building (right) and oscillator on the left. (Courtesy Jack Lewis)

towing, ferrying passengers, and picking up crabs from commercial fishermen and delivering them to Tillamook markets.

Earl Snodgrass first entered the Lighthouse Service in 1927. As was typical, his first assignment was to a remote station—Southeast Farallon Island. He and his wife stayed there about three years until he was transferred to the lighthouse at Table Bluff, overlooking Humboldt Bay. Snodgrass then quit the Lighthouse Service to accept a more lucrative job piloting boats for the Cogshaw Launch and Towboat Company. He stayed with them at Humboldt Bay for several years, finally returning to the Lighthouse Service and accepting the assignment to East Brother Island.

The assistant keeper applied his extensive experience with boats to build the first inboard motorboat used at East Brother. With its powerful Briggs and Stratton engine, it could easily buck the swift currents around the islands. Docking, which was done on the north side of the wharf, was often tricky. In his eight years on the island, Snodgrass erred

Earl Snodgrass with motorboat he built for the station. (Courtesy Jack Lewis)

Dubbed "Second Assistant" by Earl Snodgrass, McGregor waits patiently for his master to return. (Courtesy Jack Lewis)

just once in this regard. The rowboat hit the pilings, was caught by the strong tidal current, and capsized, dumping Snodgrass, his dog McGregor, and the groceries into the drink. McGregor jumped quickly onto the dock and waited patiently for his master, who had to shinny up one of the pilings. The groceries were a total loss but, fortunately, the upside-down boat was held against the wharf by the currents and did not sink.

In 1973 Jack Lewis wrote down some of his reminiscences and anecdotes of life at East Brother light station while manned by Willard Miller and his uncle:

> Every March was painting time. The entire station was painted inside and out, buff and white. You had no choice of decor, but the paint was free, and you used it profusely. Willard liked to paint the tower. He would rig a line from the tower, and when he wanted to come down he would slide down the rope and swing onto the second floor porch . . .

> Each fall before the fog season they would "fire up" the horn [diaphone] and give it a couple of blasts. Invariably there would be two or three dead sea gulls in the horns. [During the summer] they would fly in and die. Out they would come when the horn was ready for service.

With the installation of the diaphone, fresh water was no longer needed for steam boilers. Although there was now less difficulty getting enough fresh water for the station, according to Jack Lewis there was the problem of water quality:

> Their main supply was from the watershed around the cistern, the concrete slab that covers most of the island. Sea gulls were always a problem. All summer they would fly over, eat, scream, and defecate. Come the rainy season the watershed would have to be thoroughly scrubbed and the cistern cleaned. As long as I was around that was my job. Willard would lower me in a bosun's chair, and I would clean out the debris. They did not treat the water in any way. It was rain water, and if you found a crawly thing in your glass, you just didn't drink all the way to the bottom.

There was a frog in the cistern, should have brought him out. He was an albino, snow white and had no eyes. He lived there for at least five years, used to keep tabs on him. Not Calaveras caliber, but a good-sized frog.

Though Richmond and the area around Point San Pablo were growing up, the stretch of water separating East Brother from the mainland still made the island isolated.

Their only communication with the beach was an old hand-cranked phone.* Sometimes the phone worked. If it didn't, you stood out on the wharf and relied on lung power and hoped someone was listening. There was no radio, it was not considered necessary. You took the job and you understood the risks. If there was an emergency, you met it.

Before Willard Miller and Earl and Lillian Snodgrass left East Brother, they faced the most frightening event in the station's annals. The accident involved what every keeper there through the years had feared most: fire.

The morning of March 4, 1940, was one the three island residents would not soon forget. The underwater cable which usually supplied the station with power and a telephone had been disconnected for repairs. The light in the lighthouse was running off the gasoline-powered generator in the signal building. Willard Miller was on duty, keeping an eye on the generator and the light. At 2:50 A.M. the keeper grabbed his kerosene lantern and walked down to the dock to get more gasoline from one of several fifty-gallon drums stored in the boathouse. As he was filling his small container with gasoline, he stepped back and knocked over the lamp with his foot. A pool of flaming kerosene spread over the wooden floor of the boathouse. Miller tried unsuccessfully to turn off the spigot on the gasoline drum, and in so doing burned his hand and arm. He discharged the fire extinguisher, but it was too late. Almost immediately the boathouse had

*Installed in 1936.

become a raging furnace. The keeper scrambled across the wharf and up the tramway to the island. Just as he reached the top, the first of the gasoline drums exploded, sending flames 100 feet into the air.

The explosion awakened Earl and Lillian Snodgrass who, peering from their upstairs window, saw the flames reaching skyward from behind the fog signal building. They threw on some clothes and raced downstairs. By then the fire had ignited the picket fence and was soon licking at the east side of the signal building. More explosions shook the island as the fire reached the other gasoline drums. The two men sprayed the roof and side of the signal building with the garden hose but were hampered by low water pressure. With the boats gone, the telephone line out, and a wall of flames between them and Point San Pablo, all the three could do was hope that they could keep the flames from spreading across the island.

Fortunately, a night watchman on the pier at Point San

Boathouse that was destroyed in the 1940 fire. (Courtesy Jack Lewis)

One half of the island's arsenal. During World War II the station was supplied with two rifles with bayonets, and two belts of ammunition in case of enemy attack. (Courtesy Jack Lewis)

Pablo spotted the blaze. He notified the Richmond Fire Department, but they had no boats to reach the island. A fireman called the Coast Guard headquarters in San Francisco which immediately dispatched a boat with five men. The cutter roared across the bay at full throttle, taking thirty-five minutes to reach East Brother. By the time help arrived, the three island residents had battled the fire for an hour. Even with the aid of the cutter's water pump, another hour passed before the fire was finally out.

With the light of dawn, the full extent of the damage became apparent. The wharf, tramway, boathouse, and four boats lay in charred ruins. Luckily, the fog signal building, though badly scorched, survived. Had that building caught fire, the lighthouse and other structures might soon have followed. As it was, cost estimates for the damage ranged from $15,000 to $20,000, and rebuilding was not finished until June.

During World War II East Brother light station continued to perform an important role guiding ships through San

Pablo Strait, particularly with the increased ship traffic to and from Mare Island Navy Yard. To the south, the Richmond shipyards cranked out Liberty Ships in record time to help win the war.

Willard Miller stayed on as keeper until the end of June, 1942, when he retired at age sixty-five. When the Coast Guard took charge of lighthouses in 1939, he and other keepers were given the option of joining the Coast Guard and being assigned a military rank or remaining as a civilian keeper. Miller chose the latter, as did about half of the keepers around the nation. Indeed, as late as the 1970s there were still a few civilian keepers working for the Coast Guard, mostly on the East Coast.

Earl Snodgrass remained assistant at the station until 1943 when a bronchial condition forced him to move to a drier climate. Earl and Lillian Snodgrass planted the eucalyptus trees which still stand on the island, swaying in the bay breeze, quiet reminders of lighthouse life in the 1930s and early 1940s.

Aerial view of East Brother, May 11, 1945. (U.S. Coast Guard)

Saved from Destruction

After World War II, Coast Guard personnel replaced civilian keepers at East Brother. Their duties, though, remained much the same as those of their predecessors. They tended the station around the clock, watching over the light each night and, when necessary, operating the diaphone. There was still the work of cleaning the lens, checking the backup systems, doing painting and other routine maintenance work, and regularly ferrying groceries and supplies from shore to the island.

Change came slowly but surely. In 1946 use of the rainshed was discontinued, though the cistern was still used to store water delivered by the Navy. In the next few years a short-wave radio replaced the less-than-reliable telephone, and butane replaced kerosene for cooking and heating. Unfortunately, remodeling soon robbed the lighthouse exterior of much of its Victorian charm. The attractive sawn banisters of the outside stairs and balcony were replaced by simple two-by-fours and the outside walls covered with asbestos shingles.

One of the few exciting events during the 1950s occurred in 1952 when a misguided tug collided with the island in thick fog. The pilot claimed that he did not hear the diaphone. The tug company threatened to file suit against the government, assuming that the diaphone was not in operation and that the Coast Guard was negligent. A recording device attached to the signal, however, showed that it had indeed been functioning.

East Brother during the Coast Guard years. (Betty Jane Nevis Photography)

In the 1960s increases in salaries and benefits for personnel and increases in maintenance and equipment expenses brought a sharp rise in the cost of operating lighthouses. In order to lessen expenses and allow reassignment of many of the Coast Guardsmen tending lighthouses to other more critical duties, the Coast Guard in the mid 1960s launched its Lighthouse Automation Project (LAMP). The plan called for gradually automating most of the 400 remaining United States lighthouses over the next two decades.

With the initiation of LAMP, island light stations were not surprisingly given priority for automation. Ironically, East Brother was in some respects more remote now than several decades earlier. Under the Lighthouse Board and Bureau of Lighthouses most light stations were supplied by lighthouse tender. With better highways and increased automobile transportation, boat service to lighthouses was discontinued wherever possible, making island stations an even greater inconvenience.

The first announcement that East Brother would be automated came in 1967. The Coast Guard said the change-over, which would occur within two years, would include replacing the existing island buildings with a "low main-tenance structure"—namely, a steel tower or concrete block "lighthouse." Officials asserted that once the station was unmanned, a modern tower would be needed to protect the automatic light and fog signal from vandals. In the eyes of some, the quaint old lighthouse and other station buildings, so pristinely cared for through nearly a century, had outlived their usefulness. The station had survived storm waves, earthquakes, gales, collisions with ships, and a major fire, yet now seemed destined for demolition—a victim of modernization.

By 1967 the tradition of permanent residents on the island had been abandoned in favor of rotating two-man crews. The men worked forty-eight-hour shifts, exchanging duties with their partners on the mainland. The man in charge of the station was Chief Bosun's Mate Joseph Picotte. When the announcement came that the lighthouse would be automated, Picotte grew curious about its long history. He located Mrs. Annie Morisette, who still lived in nearby Richmond, and showed her one of the old journals he found that had been kept by her father, John Stenmark. This sparked many happy reminiscences for Mrs. Morisette: going to school by boat, helping raise pigs and chickens, and the courtship visits of her husband-to-be. From her Richmond home Mrs. Morisette often heard the "bee-ooh" of the diaphone, rekindling memories of the huge brass bell she used to strike as a child while her father raised steam in the boilers. Now it seemed such memories would soon be all that remained. "I'm going to miss it," she said. "It wasn't just a lighthouse to me, it was my home."[27]

During the next year, a number of history-minded area residents vowed they would somehow find a way to save the ninety-five-year-old landmark. In 1968 the newly-formed Contra Costa Shoreline Parks Committee made this one of their primary goals. At their urging, the Richmond Planning Commission, City Council, and Contra Costa County Board of Supervisors passed resolutions asking the Coast Guard to reverse its decision to demolish the buildings. The Coast Guard responded positively and in March of that year gave committee representatives and local officials a tour of the island. The Coast Guard said that it would probably be willing to donate or lease the island to any government agency wishing to preserve it as a historical landmark. Several local parks departments and the county school district expressed interest in preserving and utilizing the buildings, but none could afford the estimated high cost of maintenance coupled with the expense and inconvenience of boat service.

In July, 1969, the Coast Guard placed East Brother light station under automatic control and, for the time being, decided to let the buildings stand. To deter vandals, the windows were boarded up and the doors heavily barred. A tall chain-link fence and gate sealed off the ramp that connected the island to the dock, and "No Trespassing" signs punctuated the station's perimeter.

In early 1970 the Contra Costa Shoreline Parks Committee renewed its campaign to save East Brother. Their first goal was to have the station placed on the National Register of Historic Places. This would at least assure protection from demolition, a necessary first step before finding a new use for the buildings.

What worried the committee most was that no single agency or department was responsible for assuring the station's existence. The Coast Guard said it might still be willing to lease the property to a state or local agency, or it might turn the property over to the Bureau of Land Management or the General Services Administration. These agencies might in turn give it to a local government or sell it to a private interest. About the same time the parks committee renewed its efforts, the Bureau of Land Management burned to the ground the old keepers' dwellings of the Punta Gorda light station in Humboldt County. At least one BLM official later admitted that the burning was "probably a mistake."[28] The Punta Gorda tragedy, however, breathed new life into the campaign to preserve East Brother, before it, too, was demolished through ignorance or mistake.

In March of 1970, with the cooperation of the Coast Guard, the committee gave reporters from a San Francisco television station a tour of the island and pleaded for public support to save the lighthouse. This burst of publicity brought a flood of telephone calls, telegrams, and letters to the committee sympathetic to its efforts. Not surprisingly, several people even inquired if they could live in the lighthouse to help preserve it. Local governments and the state legislature soon passed resolutions requesting the State Department of Parks and Recreation to nominate the lighthouse to the

By 1979 the island looked like this. (Photo by Tom Butt)

National Register. On February 12, 1971, East Brother light station was finally entered on the register.

Now the problem was finding a group to restore and make use of the island facilities. Many different public agencies again expressed interest in the station, and all thought it should be utilized as a resource. However, no one was willing to foot the bill. The county school superintendent, for example, hoped that the property could be used for school and college programs in marine science and environmental studies, but these plans and others never materialized. In 1974 the abandoned lighthouse and other buildings passed the century mark in solitude. The weeds grew taller and the sun, wind, and rain began to take their toll. The island's only visitors were the Coast Guard service crews who occasionally landed to inspect the aero-beacon and electronic fog signal. The Coast Guard's budget only provided for upkeep of the navigational equipment.

In 1979, after ten years of neglect, a group of Richmond area citizens established a non-profit organization specifically dedicated to restoring the light station and making it accessible to the public. The organization, East Brother Light Station, Inc., hoped to restore the facility with the aid of grants and private donations and then maintain it through day use fees and operation as a bed and breakfast inn. The sight of the once-immaculate buildings and grounds decaying through years of abandonment brought a particular sense of urgency to the group's objectives. It seemed that this would be the last hope for restoring the landmark. Fortunately, the plan worked.

In July of 1979 the Coast Guard issued the organization a twenty-year renewable license (at no cost) to restore and occupy the station. Support came next from the U.S. Department of Interior which awarded the group a Maritime Preservation Matching Grant of $67,000. Near the end of the year, work began. It was an enormous task, primarily made

In the spring of 1980 volunteers began stripping the asbestos shingles from the lighthouse, revealing the original redwood siding and unpainted imprint where Victorian trim had been removed for "modernization." (Photo by Sylvia Malm)

Some 100 tons of concrete were hauled to the island and mixed with a small mixer to pour the new rainshed. (Photo by Sylvia Malm)

Walter Fanning, grandson of John P. Kofod (keeper from 1914 to 1921), cuts out porch railing supports during restoration. (Photo by Sylvia Malm)

possible by overwhelming community support. Individuals, businesses, corporations, and a variety of different government agencies all pitched in. Donations came in many forms: cash, building materials, services, and labor. Particularly important among the services was transportation. Small private boats, powerful tug boats, the Harbor Police patrol boat, Coast Guard buoy tenders, and East Brother's small Boston Whaler all assisted from time to time in hauling the tons of supplies and hundreds of volunteers to and from the island.

In all, over 300 people volunteered to help bring East Brother back to life. Some helped for only a day (coming partly out of curiosity); others became regulars. Each weekend, from five to twenty people were hard at work fixing up the station. The more mundane tasks included scraping old paint, puttying cracks, and chiseling off asbestos shingles. For the more skilled workers were such jobs as reconstructing the ornate woodwork or making and painting the 250 new pickets needed to repair the fence.

Soon after restoration began, it became clear that the buildings, despite their weathered exterior appearance, were for the most part structurally sound. Only the south side of the lighthouse needed new studs and sheathing. A new foundation also had to be constructed under part of the dwelling. Luckily, the station's island location had deterred most vandals and souvenir hunters while abandoned.

Not a single detail was overlooked. Through study of old photographs and the original lighthouse plans, the banisters, window trim and other fine details of the dwelling's exterior were carefully reconstructed. To learn the original colors of the lighthouse, samples of paint were analyzed by the Chevron Research Company. The machinery of the diaphone was carefully taken apart, inspected, cleaned, and reassembled. Though unused for a decade, it was in surprisingly good shape, and soon its once-familiar grunts boomed across the bay.

For the third time in the station's history, the rainshed, which had deteriorated beyond repair, had to be replaced so that rain could be captured as a water supply. First the old concrete pavement was torn up. This took a crew from the California Conservation Corps six weeks. A barge from the Army Corps of Engineers then ferried over 100 tons of concrete ready-mix to the island. Using two small electric mixers, members of a CETA-funded concrete masonry training class poured the 9,000-square-foot rainshed.

Despite occasional equipment failures, some early setbacks from rough weather, and the ambitious nature of the project, restoration was completed on time, within budget, and without any serious accidents. In November, 1980, less than a year after work began, the lighthouse was dedicated and welcomed its first overnight guests.

Today East Brother light station holds reminders of several eras. The buildings are painted much as they were in 1874 when the beacon was first lighted. The lighthouse floor plan

These before and after photos dramatically summarize the restoration story. (Photos by Sylvia Malm, above, and Frank Pedrick)

Views from the top of the lighthouse taken before and after restoration. (Photos by Sylvia Malm, above, and Frank Perry)

and location of the outside stairs reflect remodeling shortly after the turn of the century, and the fog signal equipment dates mostly from the 1930s and 1940s. There are necessarily a few modern touches too, such as new wiring, solar panels for water heating, and propane for cooking. Essentially, though, the station looks much as it did in the nineteenth century. Indeed, with a little imagination, visitors can step right back to the days of John Stenmark or Willard Miller.

Those who help operate the facility today find that the job has many similarities with the past. Of course there is the continuing battle against the natural elements. Siding has to be repainted, windows recaulked, and machinery repaired. A skilled and dedicated crew of Monday morning volunteers tends to much of this work. Without such continued volunteer support, upkeep would be a losing proposition.

Though not an official part of their duty, those working on the island keep a close watch over the bay and have several times aided boaters in distress. One afternoon a capsized

A young volunteer helps with painting. (Photo by Sylvia Malm)

canoe was sighted between East Brother and Red Rock. The light station's twenty-one-foot boat soon arrived on the scene, much to the relief of the two boaters. The two were helped aboard and taken back to the island with their canoe so that they could dry out and recover from the ordeal.

San Francisco Bay still gets fairly rough at times, precluding access to or from East Brother several days out of each year. The worst storm of recent memory struck the night of December 3, 1983. Winds of seventy-five miles per hour whipped across the bay as ten-foot waves crashed over the station wharf. The station's boat had been hoisted out of the water (with the bilge holes open) so that waves would not splash into the boat and fill it with water—at least that was the plan. The waves were so large, however, that the hull soon filled, and the added weight snapped the boat loose from the derrick. Several days later the craft's battered remains drifted ashore at Hunter's Point in San Francisco.

In December 1983 high winds whipped San Francisco Bay into a sea of waves. (Photo by a lighthouse guest)

Innkeepers Leigh and Linda Hurley admit that such incidents add spice to lighthouse life, though that one they could have lived without. The Hurleys, who are the third set of innkeepers since East Brother opened for public use, took up residence on the island in 1983 and have more than a full time job booking reservations, fixing dinner and breakfast for guests, shopping, conducting tours, cleaning, and running the boat to and from shore. Despite the traditional inconveniences, the couple cannot think of any place they would rather live. Says Mrs. Hurley, "We plan to break the Stenmarks' record and stay twenty years." The couple has already meshed well with the historical continuity of the island. A few months after moving in, they were joined by a baby daughter. With her arrival, family life returned to the island after an absence of seventy years.

Though East Brother sits in the past, it is surrounded by the present. The nearby shoreline, barren and isolated in the 1800s, supports piers, warehouses, railroad tracks, a small yacht harbor, and a Navy fuel depot. Where ferries used to transport passengers across the bay, cars speed over the four-mile-long Richmond–San Rafael Bridge. Through San Pablo Strait, where tall-masted ships once sailed, freighters carry to distant ports the harvests of California's Great Valley. But through all these changes and present emphasis on public use of the station, the lighthouse is still, and foremost, an aid to navigation.

The best part about the history of East Brother light station is that it has not yet ended. The lighthouse and other structures live on, not only guiding mariners, but also preserving part of our maritime heritage. Were it not for the many people who really cared about it and were willing to sacrifice great amounts of time and energy to preserve it, East Brother light station would not have survived into its second century. Its recent history is one of success and inspiration.

Sailboats competing in the annual Vallejo Race pass East Brother. (Photo by Sylvia Malm)

Appendices

APPENDIX A
Keepers and Assistant Keepers
East Brother Light Station
1874–1945

This list was compiled from the station journals and from the registers of lighthouse keepers' salaries. The dates of appointment were often several weeks after they began duty. The list does not include temporary and substitute keepers and assistants. Records of personnel who served on the island from 1946 to 1969 were not available.

KEEPERS

Name	Date Began Duty	Remarks
Samuel M. Farran	March 1, 1874	Resigned 1880
George B. Koons	June 27, 1880	Transferred to Point Montara October, 1880
Charles F. Winsor	October 16, 1880	Retired 1887
P. J. Quinlan	November 10, 1887	Resigned 1894
John O. Stenmark	August 31, 1894	Retired 1914
John P. Kofod	July 25, 1914	Transferred to Yerba Buena Island, 1921
Herbert Luff	May 31, 1921	
J. Dunn	October 9, 1921	
Willard Miller	November 29, 1922	Retired July, 1942
J. S. McGrath	July 2, 1942	Replaced March 1, 1944, by Acting Keeper Hall
E. P. Perry	August 14, 1944	

EAST BROTHER

Name	Date Began Duty	Remarks
John Cawley	March 1, 1874	Left the Lighthouse Service May 24, 1881
Joseph M. Page	May 28, 1881	Resigned 1883
Albert Tippett	February 10, 1883	Resigned 1886
Charles A. Paulson	April 22, 1886	Removed December 27, 1888
Charles McCarthy	February 19, 1889	Transferred and promoted to Oakland Harbor light station January, 1890
Martin Haave	January 25, 1890	Resigned September 6, 1893
James Anderson	September 8, 1893	Promoted to keeper, Point Reyes, September, 1901, and replaced temporarily by Oscar Sellman, laborer
Charles A. Paulson	November 2, 1901	Resigned from Lighthouse Service July 21, 1902, and replaced by Acting Assistant A. Bunth
John W. Astrom	September 8, 1902	
Andrew Szarnecke	August 31, 1908	
C. E. Clark	October 11, 1909	Left the Lighthouse Service February 1, 1918
E. C. Easton	February 11, 1918	
D. O. Kinyon	December 6, 1918	
W. Monette	March 6, 1919	
A. H. Joost	February 1, 1921	Promoted to keeper, Southampton Shoal, August 1921
T. F. Brown	October 10, 1921	

F. L. Pike	August 25, 1922	Resigned October 13, 1926
Roy L. Murphy	October 14, 1926	Transferred to Southeast Farallon Island September 28, 1928
Frederick S. Cobb	September 28, 1928	Promoted to keeper, Southampton Shoal, June 30, 1930
J. H. Sylvia	June 30, 1930	
W. J. Atkins	July 29, 1931	Left because of poor health 1936
Earl Snodgrass	November 30, 1936	Retired July 31, 1943
Frank Dacosta	October 1, 1943	

SECOND ASSISTANTS*

P. Moran	March 1, 1874	
James Rankin	unknown	Transferred and promoted to Fort Point August, 1878
Wm. McCarthy	August 18, 1878	Transferred to Cape Mendocino April 25, 1880

*Position of second assistant abolished at East Brother May 1, 1880.

APPENDIX B
Innkeepers under East Brother Light Station, Inc.

Pat Jackson	1980–1982
Less McDonald	1980–1981
Phil Toomire	1982–1983
Kate Toomire	1982–1983
Leigh Hurley	1983–
Linda Hurley	1983–

APPENDIX C

List of California Lighthouses

Lighthouse	County	Date Lighted	Remarks
Point Loma	San Diego	Nov. 15, 1855	Discontinued in 1891
New Point Loma	San Diego	Mar. 23, 1891	
*Ballast Point	San Diego	Aug. 1, 1890	Light relocated in 1960
Los Angeles Harbor	Los Angeles	May 7, 1912	
Point Fermin	Los Angeles	Dec. 15, 1874	Light relocated to separate tower in 1945
Point Vicente	Los Angeles	1926	
*Point Hueneme	Ventura	Dec. 5, 1874	
Anacapa Island	Ventura	1912	
*Santa Barbara	Santa Barbara	Dec. 1, 1856	Leveled by earthquake in 1926
Point Conception	Santa Barbara	Feb. 1, 1856	New lighthouse built in 1882
*Point Arguello	Santa Barbara	Feb. 22, 1901	
San Luis Obispo	San Luis Obispo	June 30, 1890	
Piedras Blancas	San Luis Obispo	Feb. 15, 1875	
Point Sur	Monterey	Aug. 1, 1889	
Point Pinos	Monterey	Feb. 1, 1855	
Point Santa Cruz	Santa Cruz	Jan. 1, 1870	Automated in 1941, new lighthouse built in 1967
*Año Nuevo Island	San Mateo	1890	Fog signal established 1872

*No longer standing

Pigeon Point	San Mateo	Nov. 15, 1872	Fog signal established 1871
Point Montara	San Mateo	Nov. 26, 1900	Fog signal established 1875
Southeast Farallon Island	San Francisco	Jan. 1, 1856	
Mile Rock	San Francisco	Feb. 15, 1906	
Fort Point	San Francisco	1855	
Alcatraz Island	San Francisco	June 1, 1854	New lighthouse built in 1909
Yerba Buena Island	San Francisco	Oct. 1, 1875	
Southampton Shoal	San Francisco	1905	Lighthouse sold and relocated in 1960
Oakland Harbor	Alameda	Jan. 27, 1890	New lighthouse built in 1903, sold and relocated in 1971
East Brother	Contra Costa	March 1, 1874	Automated in 1969
*Mare Island	Solano	1873	Discontinued in 1917
Carquinez Strait	Solano	Jan. 15, 1910	Sold and relocated in 1960s
*Roe Island	Solano	1891	Discontinued in 1945
*Angel Island (Point Knox)	Marin	1900	Fog signal established 1886
Lime Point	Marin	1900	Fog signal established 1883
Point Bonita	Marin	April 30, 1855	Lighthouse relocated in 1877
Point Reyes	Marin	Dec. 1, 1870	
Point Arena	Mendocino	May 1, 1870	New lighthouse completed in 1908
Point Cabrillo	Mendocino	June 10, 1909	

Punta Gorda	Humboldt	Jan. 15, 1912	Discontinued in 1951
Cape Mendocino	Humboldt	Dec. 1, 1868	
Table Bluff	Humboldt	Oct. 31, 1892	Discontinued in 1971
*Humboldt Harbor	Humboldt	Dec. 20, 1856	Discontinued in 1892
Trinidad Head	Humboldt	Dec. 1, 1871	
Crescent City	Del Norte	Dec. 10, 1856	Automated in 1953, discontinued in 1965
Saint George Reef	Del Norte	Oct. 20, 1892	Discontinued in 1975

Notes

1. Walton Bean, *California: An Interpretive History* (New York: McGraw-Hill, 1968), p. 197.

2. Ibid.

3. Francis Ross Holland, Jr., *The Old Point Loma Lighthouse, San Diego*, p. 12.

4. Ibid., p. 16.

5. Francis Ross Holland, Jr., *America's Lighthouses*, p. 155.

6. George R. Putnam, *Lighthouses and Lightships of the United States*, p. 100.

7. Jerry MacMullen, *Paddle-Wheel Days in California* (Stanford, California: Stanford Univ. Press, 1944), p. vii.

8. Arnold S. Lott, *A Long Line of Ships: Mare Island's Century of Naval Activity in California* (Annapolis: U.S. Naval Institute, 1954), p. 93.

9. William W. Belknap to George S. Boutwell, 28 February 1873, Record Group 26, National Archives, Washington, D.C.

10. E. J. Molera to George Elliot, 29 January 1873, collection of Society of California Pioneers, San Francisco.

11. Richard W. Updike, "Augustin Fresnel and His Lighthouse Lenses," *The Log of Mystic Seaport*, Spring 1980, p. 10.

12. Journal of the Light-House Station at East Brother Island, 19 January 1875, Record Group 26, National Archives, Washington, D.C.

13. U.S., Lighthouse Board, *Report of the United States Light-House Board*, 1876, p. 57.

14. U.S., Office of Lighthouse Inspector, Twelfth District, *Circular No. 6 of 1894*, 16 July 1894.

15. "J.O. Stenmark Answers Summons, Lighthouse Keeper Stricken Today," *Richmond Record-Herald*, 17 May 1915, p. 1.

16. Burney J. Le Boeuf and Stephanie Kaza, eds., *The Natural History*

of *Año Nuevo* (Pacific Grove, California: The Boxwood Press, 1981), p. 43.

17. "Historic Bay Lighthouse Giving Way to Progress," *Oakland Tribune,* 27 October 1967, p. 23.

18. *Richmond Record-Herald,* 8 June 1914, p. 1.

19. "Wedding Anniversary is Observed by Lightkeeper," newspaper clipping in collection of East Brother Light Station, Inc.

20. Susan D. Cole, *Richmond: Windows to the Past* (Richmond, California: Wildcat Canyon Books, 1980), p. 65.

21. F.J. Hulaniski, ed., *The History of Contra Costa County, California* (Berkeley, California: The Elms Publishing Co., 1917), p. 327.

22. U.S., Lighthouse Board, *Instructions to Light-Keepers,* July 1881, p. 30.

23. Journal of the Light-House Station at East Brother Island, 22 March 1906, Record Group 26, National Archives, Washington, D.C.

24. Putnam, op. cit., p. 127.

25. Walter Fanning, "Danish Immigrant Begins Family Tradition at East Brother," *The East Brother Light: 1982 Fundraising Edition,* p. 11. All of the quotations from Walter Fanning are taken from this article.

26. Jack Lewis to Gerald Adams, 21 May 1973. All of the quotations from Jack Lewis are from this letter, collection of East Brother Light Station, Inc.

27. "Historic Bay Lighthouse Giving Way to Progress," *Oakland Tribune,* 27 October 1967, p. 23.

28. Ralph C. Shanks, Jr. and Janetta Thompson Shanks, *Lighthouses and Lifeboats on the Redwood Coast,* p. 118.

Further Reading

Ehlers, Chad, and Gibbs, James A. *Sentinels of Solitude: West Coast Lighthouses.* Portland, Oregon: Graphic Arts Center Publishing Co., 1981. Color photos with a short history of each lighthouse.

Gibbs, James A. *Sentinels of the North Pacific.* Portland, Oregon: Binford & Mort, 1955.

Gibbs, James A. *West Coast Lighthouses.* Seattle: Superior Publishing Co., 1974. Short histories of each lighthouse with many photos.

Gibbs, James A. *Tillamook Light.* Portland, Oregon: Binford & Mort, 1979.

Holland, Francis Ross, Jr. *America's Lighthouses: Their Illustrated History Since 1716.* Brattleboro, Vermont: The Stephen Greene Press, 1972. A summary of U.S. lighthouses and lighthouse administration.

Holland, Francis Ross, Jr. *The Old Point Loma Lighthouse, San Diego.* San Diego, California: Cabrillo Historical Association, 1978. A detailed, authoritative history of this famous beacon.

Nordhoff, Charles, and Kobbe, Gustav. *The Light-houses of the United States in 1874.* Golden, Colorado: Outbooks, 1981. A collection of four articles reprinted from nineteenth century magazines with many illustrations from that period.

Perry, Frank. *Lighthouse Point: Reflections on Monterey Bay History.* Soquel, California: GBH Publishing, 1982. History of the lighthouse at Santa Cruz, California.

Putnam, George R. "Beacons of the Sea," *National Geographic*

Magazine, January 1913, pp. 1–53. Putnam headed the Bureau of Lighthouses from 1910 to 1935.

Putnam, George R. *Lighthouses and Lightships of the United States.* Boston: Houghton Mifflin Co., 1917.

Putnam, George R. "New Safeguards for Ships in Fog and Storm," *National Geographic Magazine,* August 1936, pp. 169–200.

Shanks, Ralph C., Jr., and Shanks, Janetta Thompson. *Lighthouses and Lifeboats on the Redwood Coast.* San Anselmo, California: Costaño Books, 1978.

Shanks, Ralph C., Jr., and Shanks, Janetta Thompson. *Lighthouses of San Francisco Bay.* San Anselmo, California: Costaño Books, 1976. Short histories of East Brother's neighboring beacons.

Shattuck, Clifford. *The Nubble: Cape Neddick Lightstation, York, Maine.* Freeport, Maine: The Cumberland Press, 1979.

Snow, Edward Rowe. *The Lighthouses of New England, 1716–1973.* New York: Dodd, Mead & Co., 1973. Entertaining lighthouse stories by a noted maritime historian and writer.

Stick, David. *North Carolina Lighthouses.* Raleigh: North Carolina Department of Cultural Resources, Division of Archives and History, 1980.

Strobridge, Truman R. *Chronology of Aids to Navigation and the Old Lighthouse Service 1716–1939.* Washington, D.C.: Public Affairs Division, United States Coast Guard, 1974.

United States Coast Guard. *Historically Famous Lighthouses.* Washington, D.C.: U.S. Government Printing Office, 1972. Brief histories of fifty-five U.S. lighthouses.

Principal Contributors to Restoration
($1,000 or more in materials, services, or cash, or 100 hours or more of labor)

Bruce and Sandra Beyaert
Don and Marie Blairsdale
Kurt and Elton Brombacher
Tom and Shirley Butt
Calico Corners
Chevron U.S.A.
City of Richmond Manpower
Services
City of Richmond Police
Department
Contra Costa County
Manpower Services
Tom and Lucretia Edwards
George Engeman
Phil and Sue Erickson
Pat Everitt
Walter Fanning
Lou and Jennie Fantin
Jay and Karen Fenton
Bob Fox
Vale and Louise Hammond
Fay and Marion Hawkins
Hill Lumber Company
Interactive Resources, Inc.
Maria Iwinski
Pat Jackson
L & D Scaffolds, Inc.
Sylvia Malm
P.X. Mason
McDermott-Sealy, Inc.
Less McDonald
Charles Merrill
Holbrook-Merrill
William and Sue Montague
Woody Nelson

Jerry O'Brien
Oakland Machine Works
Oceanic Society Farallones
Patrol
Frank and Pat Pearson
Doug and Karla Peterson
Plasterer's Union Local 112
Ed and Marilyn Pollock
Save San Francisco Bay
Association
Tim Slater
Soleil Realty, Inc.
Stone's Hardwood Floor
Company
Paul Strebel
Sun Light and Power
Company
The Outboard Motor Shop
U.S. Army Corps of
Engineers
U.S. Coast Guard
Bob Van Vleet
Beulah Vaughn
Carol Vieth
Jay and Barbara Vincent
Harry Weed, Jr.
Western Tug and Barge
Wayne and Sally Wheeler
Alice Widdess
Stewart Widdess

Special Thanks To

Assemblyman Bob Campbell
Congressman George Miller
Supervisor Tom Powers
Councilman Al Silva

Typesetting: Typola
Printing: Community Printers
Santa Cruz, California